CONTENTS

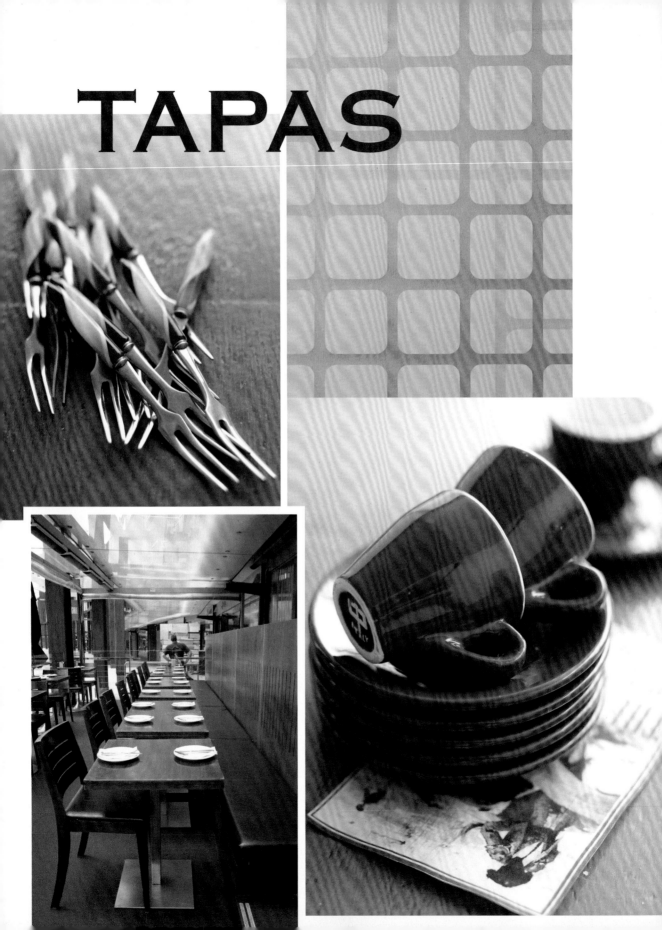

TAPAS

TAPAS

AUTHENTIC RECIPES FOR A MEDITERRANEAN FEAST

GARLIC & PAPRIKA CHAR-GRILLED PRAWNS

12 uncooked medium
    king prawns (540g)
1 medium red capsicum (bell pepper)
    (200g), chopped coarsely
⅓ cup (80ml) olive oil
2 cloves garlic, crushed
1 teaspoon smoked paprika

1 Shell and devein prawns, leaving tails intact.
2 Combine prawns, capsicum, oil, garlic and paprika in medium bowl.
3 Cook capsicum on heated grill plate until browned both sides. Add prawns towards the end of capsicum cooking time; cook, turning, until prawns are changed in colour.
4 Serve with lemon wedges, if you like.

prep + cook time 30 minutes **serves** 6
nutritional count per serving 12.5g total fat (1.8g saturated fat); 652kJ (156 cal); 1.2g carbohydrate; 9.7g protein; 0.5g fibre

ROASTED CHERRY TOMATO AND PARMESAN DIP

250g cherry tomatoes
2 teaspoons olive oil
½ cup (120g) sour cream
½ cup (40g) finely grated parmesan cheese
2 tablespoons finely chopped fresh basil
½ teaspoon dried chilli flakes
1 stick sourdough bread (200g), sliced thinly
2 cloves garlic, halved

1 Preheat oven to 220°C/200°C fan-forced.
2 Combine tomatoes and oil on oven tray. Roast, uncovered, about 15 minutes or until tomato skins split. Cool 10 minutes.
3 Combine tomatoes, sour cream, cheese, basil and chilli in medium bowl.
4 Toast bread both sides. Rub garlic onto toasts; serve with tomato and parmesan dip.

prep + cook time 35 minutes **serves** 6
nutritional count per serving 12.6g total fat (6.9g saturated fat); 932kJ (223 cal); 20g carbohydrate; 6.4g protein; 2.4g fibre

PRAWNS WITH FRESH TOMATO SAUCE

12 uncooked medium king prawns (540g)
2 tablespoons olive oil
4 cloves garlic, sliced thinly
4 medium vine-ripened tomatoes (420g),
    chopped coarsely
2 teaspoons red wine vinegar
1 tablespoon coarsely chopped fresh
    flat-leaf parsley

1 Shell and devein prawns, leaving tails intact.
2 Heat oil in large frying pan; cook garlic until browned lightly. Add tomato; cook, uncovered, stirring occasionally, about 5 minutes. Add prawns and vinegar; cook until prawns change colour. Stir in parsley.
3 Serve with crusty bread.

prep + cook time 25 minutes **serves** 6
nutritional count per serving 6.5g total fat (0.9g saturated fat); 447kJ (107 cal); 1.5g carbohydrate; 10.1g protein; 1.2g fibre

COD AND OLIVE FRITTERS

650g salted cod fillet, skin on
3 medium potatoes (600g), halved
1 tablespoon olive oil
1 medium brown onion (150g), chopped
   finely
2 cloves garlic, crushed
¼ cup finely chopped fresh flat-leaf parsley
½ cup (60g) seeded green olives, chopped
   finely
1 egg
vegetable oil, for deep-frying

1 Rinse fish under cold water to remove excess salt. Place fish in large bowl, cover with cold water; refrigerate, covered, overnight, changing the water three or four times. Drain fish; discard water.

2 Place fish in large saucepan, cover with cold water; bring to the boil uncovered. Reduce heat, simmer, covered, 5 minutes. Drain fish, discard water; remove skin and bones then flake fish.

3 Boil, steam or microwave potato until tender; drain. Roughly mash potato in large bowl.

4 Meanwhile, heat olive oil in large frying pan; cook onion and garlic, stirring, until onion softens.

5 Combine fish, onion mixture, parsley, olives and egg with potato; mix well.

6 Roll level tablespoons of fish mixture into balls, place on baking-paper-lined tray; refrigerate 30 minutes.

7 Heat vegetable oil in deep medium saucepan; deep-fry fritters, in batches, until browned lightly and heated through. Drain on absorbent paper.

prep + cook time 1 hour 30 minutes
(+ refrigeration) **makes** 40
nutritional count per fritter 2.6g total fat
(0.4g saturated fat); 196kJ (47 cal); 47.4g
carbohydrate; 3.6g protein; 0.3g fibre
Salted cod, also known as salt cod, baccalà, bacalhau, bacalao and morue, is available from Italian, Spanish and Portuguese delicatessens and some specialty food stores. It needs to be de-salted and rehydrated before use.

GRILLED MUSSELS WITH PROSCIUTTO

20 small black mussels (500g)
2 cups (500ml) water
80g butter, softened
50g thinly sliced prosciutto, chopped finely
1 clove garlic, crushed
2 green onions, chopped finely

1 Scrub mussels; remove beards. Bring the water to the boil in large saucepan. Add the mussels, cover; boil about 3 minutes or until mussels open (discard any that do not).
2 Drain mussels; discard liquid. Break open shells; discard top shell. Loosen mussels from shells with a spoon; return mussels to shells, place in single layer on oven tray.
3 Preheat grill.
4 Combine butter, prosciutto, garlic and onion in small bowl.
5 Divide butter mixture over mussels; grill about 3 minutes or until browned lightly.

prep + cook time 30 minutes **serves** 4
nutritional count per serving 17.6g total fat (11.2g saturated fat); 773kJ (185 cal); 1.8g carbohydrate; 5.5g protein; 0.2g fibre

OLIVES

Rinse and drain 370ml can anchovy-stuffed green manzanilla olives; combine in medium bowl with 1 tablespoon finely chopped fresh rosemary, 4 bay leaves, 1 tablespoon extra dry vermouth, 1 tablespoon gin and ½ cup olive oil. Cover, refrigerate overnight or up to one week. Serve olives with crusty bread.

prep time 15 minutes (+ refrigeration)

serves 8

nutritional count per serving
17.3g total fat (2.5g saturated fat); 711kJ (170 cal); 0.7g carbohydrate; 0.3g protein; 2.9g fibre

Spanish anchovy-stuffed green manzanilla olives can be found at specialty food stores.

Combine 1 cup seeded ligurian olives, 1 trimmed, thinly sliced baby fennel bulb, ½ cup fresh mint leaves, 2 tablespoons finely grated orange rind, 1 teaspoon black peppercorns and 1½ cups olive oil in medium bowl. Cover, refrigerate overnight or up to one week.

prep time 15 minutes (+ refrigeration)

serves 8

nutritional count per serving
42.9g total fat (6.1g saturated fat); 1689kJ (404 cal); 5.2g carbohydrate; 0.4g protein; 0.9g fibre

Ligurian olives are medium-sized black olives found in specialty food stores; kalamata or any other black olives can be substituted.

Combine 1¼ cups seeded kalamata olives, 1 tablespoon finely grated lemon rind, 2 halved fresh small red thai chillies, 2 garlic cloves, ¼ cup red wine vinegar and ¾ cup olive oil in medium bowl. Cover, refrigerate overnight or up to 1 week.

prep time 15 minutes (+ refrigeration)

serves 8

nutritional count per serving 21.6g total fat (3.1g saturated fat); 899kJ (215 cal); 5.6g carbohydrate; 0.2g protein; 0.5g fibre

Combine 1 cup capsicum-stuffed green olives, 2 thinly sliced garlic cloves, 1⅓ cups coarsely chopped semi-hard sheep-milk cheese, ½ teaspoon saffron threads and 1 cup olive oil in medium bowl. Cover, refrigerate overnight or up to 1 week.

prep time 15 minutes (+ refrigeration)

serves 8

nutritional count per serving 37.5g total fat (9g saturated fat); 1530kJ (366 cal); 0.5g carbohydrate; 7.4g protein; 1.6g fibre
Sheep-milk cheese can be found in specialty food stores. It can be substituted with other firm cheeses such as spanish goats cheese, provolone or mozzarella.

Combine 1¼ cups sicilian green olives, 1 cup rinsed drained caperberries, 5 sprigs fresh lemon thyme, ¼ cup sherry vinegar and ¾ cup olive oil in medium bowl. Cover, refrigerate overnight or up to 1 week.

prep time 15 minutes (+ refrigeration)

serves 8

nutritional count per serving 21.6g total fat (3.1g saturated fat); 932kJ (223 cal); 7.3g carbohydrate; 0.3g protein; 0.6g fibre

PAN-SEARED SCALLOPS WITH ANCHOVY BUTTER

2 teaspoons olive oil
12 scallops (300g), roe removed
30g butter
3 drained anchovy fillets
2 cloves garlic, crushed
2 teaspoons lemon juice
1 tablespoon finely chopped fresh chives

1   Heat oil in large frying pan; cook scallops, both sides, until browned lightly. Remove from pan; cover to keep warm.
2   Add butter, anchovies and garlic to pan; cook, stirring, until garlic is browned lightly. Return scallops to pan with juice; cook until scallops are heated through. Serve scallops drizzled with anchovy butter and sprinkled with chives.

prep + cook time 15 minutes   **serves** 4
nutritional count per serving 9.1g total fat (4.8g saturated fat); 514kJ (123 cal); 0.8g carbohydrate; 9.6g protein; 0.3g fibre

SAFFRON AND BRANDY SQUID

4 small cleaned squid hoods (300g), sliced thinly
2 cloves garlic, crushed
pinch saffron threads
2 teaspoons hot water
1 tablespoon olive oil
2 tablespoons brandy
100g baby spinach leaves

1 Combine squid and garlic in medium bowl.
2 Place saffron in small dish; stir in the water.
3 Heat oil in large frying pan; cook squid until browned lightly, remove from pan.
4 Add brandy to pan; cook about 30 seconds or until brandy has almost evaporated.
5 Add spinach and saffron to pan; cook, stirring, until spinach is wilted. Return squid to pan; mix gently. Serve immediately.

prep + cook time 10 minutes **serves** 4
nutritional count per serving 5.6g total fat (1g saturated fat); 527kJ (126 cal); 0.3g carbohydrate; 13.2g protein; 0.9g fibre

 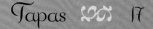

CHICKEN, RAISIN AND PINE NUT EMPANADAS

1 litre (4 cups) water

1 chicken breast fillet (200g)

2 teaspoons olive oil

1 small brown onion (80g), chopped finely

2 cloves garlic, crushed

½ can (205g) crushed tomatoes

1 bay leaf

¼ teaspoon dried chilli flakes

2 tablespoons raisins, chopped coarsely

2 tablespoons pine nuts, roasted

½ teaspoon ground cinnamon

2 tablespoons finely chopped fresh
    flat-leaf parsley

1 egg

pastry

1⅔ cups (250g) plain flour

150g cold butter, chopped

1 egg

1 tablespoon cold water

1 Bring the water to the boil in medium saucepan; add chicken, return to the boil. Reduce heat; simmer, covered, about 10 minutes or until chicken is cooked through. Cool chicken in poaching liquid 10 minutes. Remove chicken from pan; discard poaching liquid. Shred chicken finely.

2 Heat oil in medium frying pan; cook onion and garlic, stirring, until onion softens. Add undrained tomato, bay leaf and chilli; cook, stirring occasionally, about 5 minutes or until mixture thickens.

3 Add chicken, raisins, nuts and cinnamon to tomato mixture; stir until heated through. Stir in parsley. Cool mixture, covered, in the refrigerator.

4 Meanwhile, make pastry.

5 Preheat oven to 200°C/180°C fan-forced.

6 Roll one pastry half between sheets of baking paper until 2mm thick; using 10cm-round cutter, cut 10 rounds from pastry.

7 Place 1 level tablespoon of chicken mixture in centre of each round; fold round in half to enclose filling, pinching edges to seal. Press around edges of empanadas with a fork. Repeat with remaining pastry half and chicken mixture to make a total of 20 empanadas, re-rolling pastry scraps as required.

8 Place empanadas on baking-paper-lined oven trays; brush with egg. Bake 20 minutes or until browned lightly.

pastry Process flour and butter until crumbly. Add egg and the water; process until mixture comes together. Knead dough on floured surface until smooth. Divide in half, enclose in plastic wrap; refrigerate 30 minutes.

prep + cook time 2 hours (+ refrigeration)

makes 20

nutritional count per empanada 8.9g total fat (4.5g saturated fat); 594kJ (142 cal); 10.6g carbohydrate; 4.6g protein; 0.9g fibre

POTATO, DILL AND PRAWN TORTILLA

30g butter
2 teaspoons olive oil
2 medium potatoes (400g), chopped finely
1 medium brown onion (150g), chopped finely
12 uncooked medium king prawns (540g)
6 eggs
2 tablespoons sour cream
2 tablespoons finely chopped fresh dill

1 Preheat oven to 200°C/180°C fan-forced.
2 Heat butter and oil in medium frying pan; cook potato, stirring occasionally, 5 minutes. Add onion; cook, stirring occasionally, until potato is browned and tender.
3 Meanwhile, shell and devein prawns; add to pan with potato. Cook until prawns change colour.
4 Whisk eggs with sour cream in medium bowl until smooth; stir in dill. Pour mixture into pan; stir gently. Cook tortilla over low heat, about 10 minutes or until bottom sets. Wrap pan handle in foil; place pan in oven. Cook tortilla, uncovered, about 15 minutes or until tortilla is set and browned.
5 Stand tortilla 10 minutes before cutting into bite size pieces; serve warm.

prep + cook time 45 minutes **serves** 10
nutritional count per serving 8.3g total fat (3.8g saturated fat); 589kJ (141 cal); 5.5g carbohydrate; 10.7g protein; 0.8g fibre

SHERRY-GLAZED CHICKEN LIVERS

1 tablespoon olive oil

500g chicken livers, trimmed, sliced thinly

20g butter

2 shallots (50g), chopped finely

⅓ cup (80ml) dry sherry

½ cup (125ml) chicken stock

2 small long crusty bread rolls (120g),
    sliced into 6 slices each

30g watercress sprigs

1 teaspoon sherry vinegar

1 Heat oil in large frying pan; add liver, stir over high heat about 1 minute or until liver is barely cooked. Remove from pan; cover to keep warm.

2 Add butter and shallot to same pan; cook, stirring, until shallot softens.

3 Add sherry to pan; simmer until liquid is reduced by half. Add stock; simmer until liquid is slightly thickened. Return liver to pan; stir until heated.

4 Toast bread rolls lightly both sides.

5 Spoon liver mixture over toast; sprinkle watercress with vinegar. Top toasts with watercress mixture.

prep + cook time 30 minutes **makes** 12
nutritional count per piece 4.9g total fat (1.7g saturated fat); 464kJ (111 cal); 6.1g carbohydrate; 8.7g protein; 0.5g fibre

LEMON AND CHILLI CHICKEN SKEWERS

400g chicken breast fillets, cut into 2cm
   pieces
2 chorizo (340g), cut into 2cm pieces
1 medium yellow capsicum (200g),
   cut into 2cm pieces
12 bay leaves
1 tablespoon finely grated lemon rind
1 tablespoon lemon juice
¼ cup (60ml) olive oil
2 cloves garlic, crushed
1 teaspoon dried chilli flakes
¼ cup finely chopped fresh flat-leaf parsley.

1 Combine ingredients in large bowl; cover, refrigerate 30 minutes.

2 Thread chicken, chorizo, capsicum and bay leaves, alternately, onto skewers.

3 Cook skewers on heated oiled grill plate (or grill or barbecue) until chicken is cooked through and chorizo is browned lightly.

prep + cook time 30 minutes (+ refrigeration)
makes 12
nutritional count per skewer 15.3g total fat (4.4g saturated fat); 832kJ (199 cal); 1.3g carbohydrate; 14.3g protein; 0.4g fibre
Soak 12 bamboo skewers in water for at least an hour before using to prevent them from scorching during cooking.

FENNEL AND GARLIC ROASTED PORK RIBS

1 tablespoon fennel seeds
⅓ cup (90g) tomato purée
1 tablespoon brown sugar
¼ cup (60ml) sherry vinegar
4 cloves garlic, crushed
2 teaspoons smoked paprika
¼ cup (60ml) olive oil
2 x 500g racks pork spare ribs

1 Combine seeds, purée, sugar, vinegar, garlic, paprika and oil in medium jug. Reserve ¼ cup of the marinade. Place pork in shallow dish, pour over marinade; turn pork to coat in marinade. Cover; refrigerate 1 hour.
2 Preheat oven to 200°C/180°C fan-forced.
3 Place pork on oiled wire rack over large baking dish; roast, uncovered, 30 minutes.
4 Increase oven temperature to 220°C/200°C fan-forced. Brush pork with reserved marinade; roast about 20 minutes or until cooked through.
5 Slice ribs between the bones; serve with lemon wedges, if you like.

fennel and garlic roasted pork ribs

prep + cook time 1 hour (+ refrigeration)
serves 6
nutritional count per serving 15.2g total fat (3.3g saturated fat); 915kJ (219 cal); 3.9g carbohydrate; 16.5g protein; 1g fibre

VEAL MEATBALLS WITH GAZPACHO SALSA

1 tablespoon olive oil
1 large brown onion (200g), chopped finely
2 cloves garlic, crushed
500g veal mince
2 tablespoons finely chopped fresh oregano
1½ cups (120g) finely grated manchego
    cheese
1 cup (70g) stale breadcrumbs
1 egg
vegetable oil, for shallow-frying
gazpacho salsa
1 lebanese cucumber (130g), seeded,
    chopped finely
1 medium green capsicum (200g),
    chopped finely
½ small red onion (50g), chopped finely
1 small tomato (30g), seeded, chopped finely
2 tablespoons olive oil
1 tablespoon sherry vinegar

1 Make gazpacho salsa.
2 Heat olive oil in medium frying pan; cook
onion and garlic, stirring, until onion softens.
Cool 5 minutes.
3 Combine onion mixture, veal, oregano, cheese,
breadcrumbs and egg in large bowl. Roll rounded
tablespoons of the veal mixture into balls.
4 Heat vegetable oil in large frying pan; shallow-fry
meatballs, in batches, until cooked through. Drain
on absorbent paper. Serve hot with gazpacho
salsa.

veal meatballs with gazpacho salsa

gazpacho salsa Combine ingredients in small
bowl.

prep + cook time 50 minutes **makes** 40
nutritional count per meatball 4.1g total fat
(1.1g saturated fat); 247kJ (59 cal); 1.7g
carbohydrate; 3.7g protein; 0.3g fibre
*Manchego cheese is a sharp, firm spanish
cheese; it can be found in most specialty food
stores. You can use parmesan cheese instead, if
manchego is not available.*

 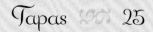

BITES

caramelised tomato and ham bites Cook 2 finely chopped shallots in heated oiled medium frying pan until soft. Add 250g halved cherry tomatoes; cook 5 minutes. Add ¼ cup balsamic vinegar and 1 tablespoon brown sugar; cook, stirring occasionally, until thickened. Cut 1 brioche loaf into 16 slices; cut 32 x 6.5cm rounds from slices. Top half the slices with 2 cups finely grated semi-hard sheep-milk cheese; grill until cheese melts. Toast remaining rounds until golden. Divide 185g thinly sliced double smoked leg ham among toast rounds; top each with caramelised tomatoes, top with remaining toasts. Serve warm.

prep + cook time 40 minutes
makes 16
nutritional count per bite
7.5g total fat (4.1g saturated fat); 644kJ (154 cal); 12.7g carbohydrate; 8.4g protein; 0.7g fibre

prawn and caper sandwiches
Combine 300g cooked, shelled, finely chopped prawns, ¼ cup rinsed drained, finely chopped capers,
1 cup mayonnaise, 1 teaspoon sweet paprika, ¼ cup finely chopped fresh flat-leaf parsley and 1 crushed garlic clove in medium bowl. Divide prawn mixture between 9 slices of white bread; top with another 9 slices bread. Trim crusts; cut each sandwich into four triangles.

prep time 30 minutes
makes 36
nutritional count per triangle
2.6g total fat (0.3g saturated fat); 255kJ (61 cal); 7g carbohydrate; 2.1g protein; 0.4g fibre

asparagus and coppa salad bites Boil, steam or microwave 170g trimmed asparagus, drain. Finely chop asparagus; combine with 1 finely chopped small red onion, 2 tablespoons finely chopped fresh basil, 2 teaspoons red wine vinegar and 2 tablespoons olive oil in medium bowl. Split 10 mini croissants in half. Divide 200g thinly sliced coppa among half the croissants; top with asparagus mixture, then remaining croissant halves. Serve at room temperature.

prep time 15 minutes
makes 10
nutritional count per bite
11.4g total fat (4.6g saturated fat); 744kJ (178 cal); 11.5g carbohydrate; 6.9g protein; 1.1g fibre

chicken, almond and tarragon mini rolls Combine 200g cooked finely shredded chicken breast fillet, ⅓ cup finely chopped fresh tarragon, ¼ cup roasted slivered almonds, 1 trimmed finely chopped celery stalk, 3 finely chopped green onions and ⅓ cup mayonnaise in medium bowl. Make a cut in tops of 12 mini bread rolls. Spoon chicken mixture into bread rolls.

prep time 20 minutes
makes 12
nutritional count per roll
5.7g total fat (0.7g saturated fat); 660kJ (158 cal); 17.5g carbohydrate; 8.2g protein; 1.7g fibre
Chicken mixture can be made one day ahead; keep, covered, in the refrigerator.

blue cheese and fig bites
Process ⅓ cup roasted slivered almonds with 2 coarsely chopped green onions, 1 cup loosely packed fresh mint leaves, ⅓ cup olive oil and 1 tablespoon lemon juice until smooth. Halve 1 long turkish loaf lengthways; cut each half lengthways into 3 fingers then cut fingers into four crossways to get 24 slices. Toast bread under hot grill. Spread almond mixture on half the toasts; top with 200g thinly sliced semi-dried figs and 100g thinly sliced blue cheese. Top with remaining toast; serve warm.

prep + cook time 20 minutes
makes 12
nutritional count per bite
11.9g total fat (2.9g saturated fat); 1012kJ (242 cal); 25.5g carbohydrate; 6.2g protein; 3.9g fibre

ARTICHOKE AND ASPARAGUS FRITTERS WITH OLIVE RELISH

170g asparagus, trimmed, chopped finely
280g jar artichokes in brine, drained,
    chopped finely
2 eggs
2 tablespoons finely chopped fresh mint
½ cup (40g) finely grated parmesan cheese
¼ cup (35g) self-raising flour
vegetable oil, for shallow frying
olive relish
½ cup (60g) seeded green olives,
    chopped finely
½ cup (60g) seeded black olives,
    chopped finely
¼ cup finely chopped fresh flat-leaf parsley
1 tablespoon finely chopped fresh chives
1 tablespoon olive oil
1 tablespoon lemon juice

1 Make olive relish.
2 Combine asparagus, artichoke, eggs, mint, cheese and flour in medium bowl.
3 Heat oil in large frying pan; shallow-fry heaped tablespoons of fritter mixture, in batches, until browned all over and cooked through. Drain fritters on absorbent paper; serve hot with olive relish.

olive relish Combine ingredients in small bowl.

prep + cook time 40 minutes **makes** 15
nutritional count per fritter 4.6g total fat
(1.2g saturated fat); 288kJ (69 cal); 3.8g
carbohydrate; 2.9g protein; 0.8g fibre

GRILLED EGGPLANT WITH MARJORAM VINAIGRETTE

1 large eggplant (500g), sliced into
  5mm rounds

¼ cup (60ml) olive oil

1 small red onion (100g), sliced thinly

¼ cup (60ml) sherry vinegar

2 teaspoons caster sugar

2 tablespoons finely chopped fresh
  marjoram

½ cup (125ml) olive oil, extra

1 Preheat oven to 200°C/180°C fan-forced.

2 Brush both sides of eggplant slices with oil; place, in single layer, on baking-paper-lined oven trays. Bake about 25 minutes, turning eggplant slices once, until browned lightly both sides.

3 Meanwhile, combine onion, vinegar, sugar, marjoram and extra oil in small bowl; spoon over eggplant.

4 Serve warm or at room temperature with crusty bread.

prep + cook time 50 minutes **serves** 6
nutritional count per serving 28.3g total fat (4g saturated fat); 1112kJ (278 cal); 4.6g carbohydrate; 1.2g protein; 2.2g fibre

ANCHOVY AND GOATS CHEESE BAKED MUSHROOMS

20 large button mushrooms (400g)
1¾ cup (120g) stale breadcrumbs
120g soft goats cheese
¼ cup (60ml) olive oil
4 drained anchovy fillets, chopped finely
⅓ cup finely chopped fresh chives
1 cup (250ml) chicken stock

1 Preheat oven to 200°C/180°C fan-forced.
2 Remove and discard stems from mushrooms; place mushroom caps, in single layer, in medium baking dish.
3 Combine breadcrumbs, cheese, oil, anchovy and chives in medium bowl. Stuff mushrooms with mixture.
4 Add stock to baking dish; bake, uncovered, about 15 minutes or until mushrooms are browned lightly.

prep + cook time 40 minutes **makes** 20
nutritional count per mushroom 4.1g total fat (1.1g saturated fat); 276kJ (66 cal); 4.3g carbohydrate; 2.7g protein; 0.8g fibre

ROASTED THYME POTATOES WITH SPICY SAUCE

500g baby new potatoes, halved
2 tablespoons olive oil
1 tablespoon finely chopped fresh thyme
spicy sauce
1 tablespoon olive oil
1 small brown onion (80g), chopped finely
2 cloves garlic, sliced thinly
1 fresh small red thai chilli, chopped finely
410g can crushed tomatoes
2 teaspoons caster sugar

1　Preheat oven to 220°C/200°C fan-forced.
2　Combine potatoes, oil and thyme in large baking dish; roast about 30 minutes or until potato is tender.
3　Meanwhile, make spicy sauce.
4　Serve spicy sauce with hot roasted potatoes.
spicy sauce　Heat oil in medium saucepan; cook onion, garlic and chilli, stirring occasionally, until onion is soft. Add undrained tomatoes and sugar; bring to the boil. Reduce heat; simmer, uncovered, stirring occasionally, about 10 minutes or until sauce thickens.

prep + cook time 45 minutes　**serves** 8
nutritional count per serving 7g total fat (1g saturated fat); 506kJ (121 cal); 11.5g carbohydrate; 2.1g protein; 2.2g fibre

ROSEMARY POTATOES WITH LEEK AND CHORIZO

500g baby new potatoes, sliced thickly
2 chorizo (340g), cut into 1-cm thick slices
1 large leek (500g), trimmed, chopped
   coarsely
6 cloves garlic
1 tablespoon finely chopped fresh rosemary
2 teaspoons sweet paprika
5 bay leaves
¼ cup (60ml) olive oil

1 Preheat oven to 220°C/200°C fan-forced.
2 Combine ingredients in large baking dish.
Roast, uncovered, about 30 minutes or until
potatoes are browned lightly.

prep + cook time 45 minutes **serves** 8
nutritional count per serving 19.8g total fat
(5.6g saturated fat); 1120kJ (268 cal); 11g
carbohydrate; 10.6g protein; 2.9g fibre

BRAISED ARTICHOKES WITH CRUNCHY ALMOND TOPPING

6 large globe artichokes (2.4kg)
4 bay leaves
4 cloves garlic
1 litre (4 cups) chicken stock
crunchy almond topping
¾ cup (50g) stale breadcrumbs
⅓ cup (25g) flaked almonds
2 tablespoons finely chopped fresh
    flat-leaf parsley
½ cup (60g) seeded green olives,
    chopped finely
¼ cup (60ml) olive oil
1 tablespoon finely grated lemon rind
2 tablespoons lemon juice

1 Preheat oven to 200°C/180°C fan-forced.
2 Prepare artichokes by snapping off tough outer leaves and peeling stems. Trim stems to 5cm. Cut 2cm off top of artichokes to reveal chokes. Cut artichokes in half from top to bottom, then scoop out and discard furry chokes from the centres. As you finish preparing each artichoke, place it in a large bowl of water containing the juice of about half a lemon (this stops any discolouration while you are preparing the next one).
3 Drain artichokes. Combine artichokes, bay leaves, garlic and stock in small baking dish, ensuring artichokes are covered with stock. Bake, covered, 45 minutes or until artichokes are tender.
4 Meanwhile, make crunchy almond topping.
5 Drain artichokes; discard liquid.
6 Serve artichokes hot or at room temperature sprinkled with crunchy almond topping.
crunchy almond topping Combine breadcrumbs and nuts on oven tray; roast about 5 minutes, cool 5 minutes. Combine breadcrumb mixture with remaining ingredients in small bowl.

prep + cook time 1 hour 40 minutes **serves** 6
nutritional count per serving 13.1g total fat (1.9g saturated fat); 928kJ (222 cal); 13.1g carbohydrate; 11.6g protein; 3.3g fibre

SMOKED EGGPLANT
AND CAPSICUM JAM

1 large eggplant (500g), chopped finely
1 medium red capsicum (bell pepper) (200g),
   chopped finely
1 medium red onion (170g), chopped finely
¼ cup (60ml) olive oil
1 tablespoon fresh thyme leaves
1 tablespoon smoked paprika
¼ teaspoon cayenne pepper
¼ cup (60ml) lemon juice
½ cup (125ml) water

1 Preheat oven to 220°C/200°C fan-forced.
2 Combine eggplant, capsicum, onion and oil on
baking-paper-lined oven tray; roast, uncovered,
about 30 minutes or until vegetables are browned
lightly.
3 Combine roasted vegetables, thyme, paprika,
pepper, juice and the water in medium saucepan.
Bring to the boil; reduce heat, simmer, uncovered,
about 15 minutes or until jam is thickened.
4 Serve jam, warm or at room temperature, with
char-grilled pitta bread.

prep + cook time 1 hour **serves** 8
nutritional count per serving 7.1g total fat (1g
saturated fat); 364kJ (87 cal); 3.8g carbohydrate;
1.4g protein; 2g fibre
*Smoked eggplant and capsicum jam can be
tossed through pasta, spread on pizza bases,
or served as side dish to chicken, lamb or fish.*

PICKLED QUAIL EGGS AND BEETROOT

12 quail eggs
500g baby beetroot, leaves trimmed
1 litre (4 cups) cider vinegar
¾ cup (165g) caster sugar
2 bay leaves
1 tablespoon black peppercorns
2 teaspoons finely grated fresh horseradish
¼ cup lightly packed fresh dill leaves

1 Sterilise 1.25-litre (5-cup) jar and lid.
2 Add eggs to small saucepan of boiling water; simmer, uncovered, about 6 minutes. Drain, then shell eggs.
3 Trim leaves from beetroot; place unpeeled beetroot in large saucepan of boiling water. Boil, covered, about 20 minutes or until beetroot are tender. Cool beetroot 10 minutes then peel.
4 Combine vinegar, sugar, bay leaves, peppercorns and horseradish in medium saucepan; stir over heat until sugar dissolves then bring to the boil. Remove from heat, stir in dill.
5 Place eggs and beetroot in hot sterilised jar; pour in enough vinegar mixture to cover eggs and beetroot. Seal jar; cool. Refrigerate overnight or for up to 1 week.

prep + cook time 1 hour (+ refrigeration)
serves 6
nutritional count per serving 1.9g total fat (0.6g saturated fat); 736kJ (176 cal); 33.9g carbohydrate; 4g protein; 2.5g fibre
Wear disposable gloves when handling the cooked beetroot. If you squeeze the warm beetroot, the skin should burst and peel away easily.
Quail eggs are available from specialty food stores and some poultry shops. Fresh horseradish is available from most greengrocers.

BROAD BEANS AND THYME

600g frozen broad beans, thawed
10g butter
2 shallots (50g), chopped finely
150g speck, chopped finely
1 tablespoon fresh thyme leaves
1 tablespoon lemon juice

1 Drop beans into medium saucepan of boiling water, return to the boil; drain. When beans are cool enough to handle, peel away grey-coloured outer shells.
2 Heat butter in large frying pan; cook shallot and speck, stirring, until speck is browned lightly. Add beans and thyme; cook, stirring, until beans are heated through. Stir in juice.

prep + cook time 40 minutes **serves** 4
nutritional count per serving 7.7g total fat (3.5g saturated fat); 589kJ (141 cal); 2g carbohydrate; 13.9g protein; 4.8g fibre

CHORIZO AND CHICKPEAS IN WHITE WINE

1 tablespoon olive oil
1 small brown onion (80g), sliced finely
2 cloves garlic, crushed
2 chorizo (340g), chopped coarsely
1 medium red capsicum (bell pepper) (200g), sliced finely
400g can chickpeas, rinsed, drained
½ teaspoon smoked paprika
¼ cup (60ml) dry white wine
⅓ cup (80ml) chicken stock

1 Heat oil in large frying pan; cook onion, garlic and chorizo, stirring, until chorizo is browned lightly.
2 Add capsicum, chickpeas and paprika; cook, stirring, until capsicum softens. Add wine and stock; cook, stirring, until liquid is reduced by half.

prep + cook time 25 minutes **serves** 6
nutritional count per serving 21.1g total fat (6.8g saturated fat); 1241kJ (297 cal); 9.6g carbohydrate; 14.6g protein; 3g fibre

broad beans and thyme

chorizo and chickpeas in white wine

 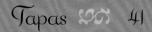

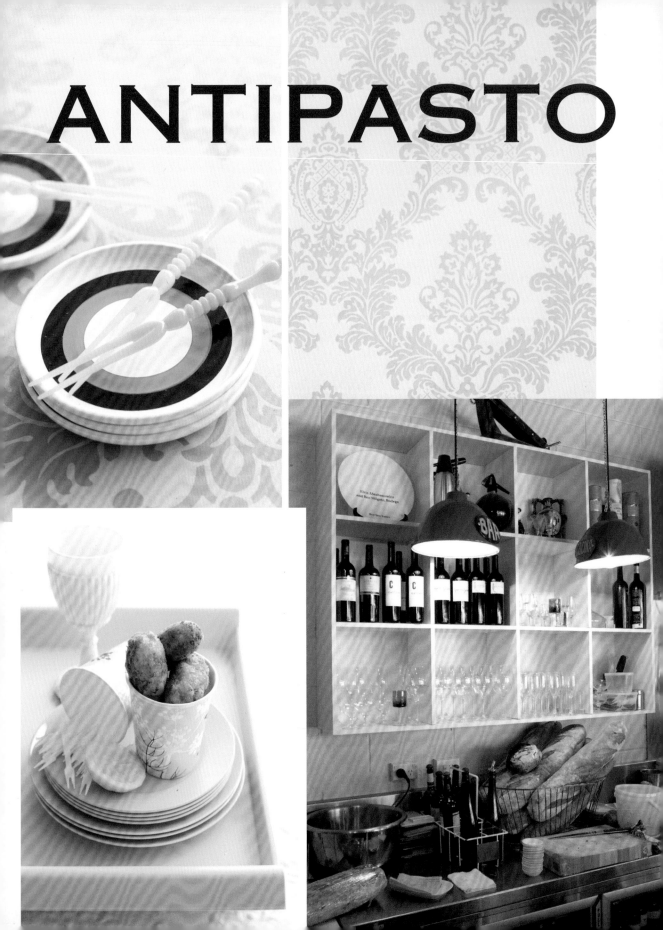

ANTIPASTO

GIARDINIERA

2 medium red capsicums (bell peppers)
   (400g)
1 litre (4 cups) white vinegar
2 cups (500ml) water
6 black peppercorns
1 bay leaf
1 tablespoon sea salt flakes
1 small eggplant (courgette) (230g),
   quartered lengthways,
   cut into 1cm slices
½ small cauliflower (200g), cut into florets
2 medium carrots (240g), sliced thinly
   diagonally
2 stalks celery (300g), trimmed,
   sliced thickly diagonally
2 tablespoons finely chopped fresh
   flat-leaf parsley
2 teaspoons finely chopped fresh thyme
2 cups (500ml) olive oil
2 cloves garlic, sliced thinly

1 Preheat oven to 200°C/180°C fan-forced. Sterilise 1.5-litre (6-cup) jar and lid.
2 Quarter capsicums; discard seeds and membranes. Roast capsicum, skin-side up, until skin blisters and blackens. Cover capsicum with plastic or paper for 5 minutes; peel away skin then slice thickly.
3 Meanwhile, combine vinegar, the water, peppercorns, bay leaf and half the salt in large saucepan; heat without boiling. Add eggplant, cauliflower, carrot and celery; bring to the boil. Reduce heat; simmer, uncovered, about 5 minutes or until vegetables are tender. Drain vegetables; discard liquid.
4 Combine hot vegetables, capsicum, herbs and remaining salt in large heatproof bowl. Spoon vegetable mixture into sterilised jar.
5 Heat oil and garlic in small saucepan, strain into large heatproof jug; discard garlic. Carefully pour hot oil over vegetables in jar to completely cover vegetables, leaving a 1cm space between vegetables and top of jar. Seal while hot.

prep + cook time 1 hour **makes** 6 cups
nutritional count per ¼ cup 19.1g total fat (2.7g saturated fat); 748kJ (179 cal); 1.6g carbohydrate; 0.7g protein; 1g fibre
Derived from an Italian word meaning 'garden', giardiniera is an Italian dish of pickled vegetables, often served as part of an antipasto platter. Store in the refrigerator for up to three months. Serve with crusty bread or as part of an antipasto platter with cheeses and deli meats.

ROASTED FENNEL DIP

4 baby fennel bulbs with fronds (520g)
2 cloves garlic, unpeeled
1 tablespoon olive oil
1 cup (240g) sour cream

1 Preheat oven to 200°C/180°C fan-forced.
2 Halve fennel lengthways; remove and discard cores. Reserve 2 teaspoons coarsely chopped fennel fronds.
3 Combine fennel, garlic and oil in small baking dish; roast, uncovered, about 30 minutes or until fennel is tender. Cool.
4 Peel garlic; blend or process fennel, garlic and sour cream until smooth. Serve dip sprinkled with reserved fennel fronds.

prep + cook time 45 minutes **makes** 1½ cups
nutritional count per teaspoon 1.6g total fat (0.9g saturated fat); 67kJ (16 cal); 0.2g carbohydrate; 0.1g protein; 0.1g fibre
serve with garlic pizza wedges, see page 51.

WHITE BEAN DIP

1 tablespoon olive oil
1 medium leek (350g), sliced thinly
400g can white beans, rinsed, drained
300ml cream
1 teaspoon finely grated lemon rind
1 tablespoon lemon juice
2 tablespoons finely chopped fresh flat-leaf
   parsley

prep + cook time 25 minutes **makes** 2½ cups
nutritional count per teaspoon 1.2g total fat
(0.7g saturated fat); 59kJ (14 cal); 0.4g
carbohydrate; 0.2g protein; 0.2g fibre
*We used cannellini beans in this recipe but you
can use any white bean you like.*

1 Heat oil in small frying pan; cook leek, stirring,
about 10 minutes or until leek softens. Cool.
2 Blend or process leek, beans, cream, rind
and juice until smooth. Stir in parsley. Serve with
crusty bread.

ROASTED CAPSICUM AND WALNUT DIP

2 medium red capsicums (bell peppers) (400g)
250g cream cheese
½ cup (60g) finely chopped roasted walnuts

1 Preheat oven to 220°C/200°C fan-forced.
2 Quarter capsicums; discard seeds and membranes. Roast, skin-side up, until skin blisters and blackens. Cover capsicum with plastic or paper for 5 minutes; peel away skin, then chop coarsely.
3 Blend or process capsicum and cream cheese until smooth; stir in nuts.

prep + cook time 40 minutes **makes** 2 cups
nutritional count per teaspoon 1.3g total fat (0.6g saturated fat); 59kJ (14 cal); 0.2g carbohydrate; 0.4g protein; 0.1g fibre
serve with garlic pizza wedges, see page 51.

CHUNKY OLIVE
AND HERB DIP

½ cup (80g) finely chopped seeded green
olives
½ cup finely chopped fresh flat-leaf parsley
½ cup finely chopped fresh mint
¼ cup finely chopped fresh dill
6 drained anchovy fillets, chopped finely
2 teaspoons finely grated lemon rind
¼ cup (60ml) lemon juice
½ cup (125ml) olive oil

1 Combine ingredients in medium bowl.

prep time 20 minutes **makes** 1½ cups
nutritional count per teaspoon 1.6g total fat
(0.2g saturated fat); 67kJ (16 cal); 0.3g
carbohydrate; 0.1g protein; 0.1g fibre
serve with garlic pizza wedges, see page 51.

GARLIC PIZZA WEDGES

1 cup (250ml) warm water
1 teaspoon caster sugar
7g sachet dried yeast
2½ cups (375g) plain flour
1 teaspoon salt
1 tablespoon olive oil
2 cloves garlic, crushed
2 tablespoons finely grated parmesan
   cheese

1 Combine the water, sugar and yeast in small jug. Stand in warm place about 10 minutes or until frothy.

2 Sift flour and salt into large bowl. Add yeast mixture; mix to a soft dough. Knead dough on floured surface about 10 minutes or until smooth and elastic. Place dough in oiled large bowl; cover. Stand in warm place about 1 hour or until dough is doubled in size.

3 Preheat oven to 220°C/200°C fan-forced. Grease two oven or pizza trays.

4 Divide dough in half. Roll each portion into a 30cm round; place on trays.

5 Brush pizza bases with combined oil and garlic; sprinkle with cheese.

6 Bake pizzas about 20 minutes or until browned and crisp. Cut each pizza into 16 wedges.

prep + cook time 1 hour (+ standing)
makes 32
nutritional count per wedge 0.9g total fat (0.2g saturated fat); 209kJ (50 cal); 8.6g carbohydrate; 1.5g protein; 0.5g fibre
This recipe is a good accompaniment for the dips in this book.

STUFFED BABY CAPSICUMS

24 vine sweet minicap baby capsicums (bell peppers) (350g)
250g ricotta cheese
2 tablespoons finely grated parmesan cheese
2 tablespoons coarsely chopped roasted pine nuts
4 slices hot salami (40g), chopped finely
2 tablespoons finely chopped fresh oregano

1 Preheat oven to 200°C/180°C fan-forced.
2 Carefully cut tops from capsicums; reserve tops. Scoop out and discard seeds and membranes.
3 Combine remaining ingredients in small bowl. Place mixture in medium piping bag fitted with 1cm plain tube. Pipe filling into capsicums; replace tops. Place capsicums, in single layer, in oiled medium shallow baking dish.
4 Roast capsicums about 20 minutes or until tender. Serve hot or cold.

prep + cook time 1 hour **makes** 24
nutritional count per capsicum 2.6g total fat (1g saturated fat); 138kJ (33 cal); 0.5g carbohydrate; 1.9g protein; 0.2g fibre
You will need about two packets of vine sweet minicaps for this recipe. Vine sweet minicaps can be orange, red or yellow and are about the size of baby red capsicums. They're flavoursome with a crispy texture; they have a very fine skin, but still need deseeding. We used sopressa siciliana salami in this recipe.

CARPACCIO

salmon carpaccio Tightly wrap 400g piece sashimi salmon in plastic wrap; freeze 1 hour. Unwrap salmon; slice thinly. Arrange slices on serving platter; drizzle with 2 tablespoons white wine vinegar. Refrigerate 1 hour. Slice 2 baby fennel bulbs thinly. Reserve 2 teaspoons finely chopped fennel fronds. Combine fennel, fronds, 2 teaspoons finely grated orange rind, ¼ cup orange juice, 1 tablespoon olive oil and 1 teaspoon finely chopped fresh thyme in medium bowl. Drain excess vinegar from salmon; serve topped with fennel mixture.
prep time 30 minutes (+ freezing and refrigeration) **serves** 8
nutritional count per serving 5.9g total fat (1.1g saturated fat); 414kJ (99 cal); 1.3g carbohydrate; 10g protein; 0.6g fibre

zucchini carpaccio Using vegetable peeler, slice 3 large zucchinis (courgettes) lengthways into ribbons. Combine zucchini in medium bowl with 2 tablespoons olive oil, ¼ cup white wine vinegar, 2 teaspoons caster sugar, 2 tablespoons finely chopped fresh chives and 1 seeded, finely chopped medium egg tomato. Cover; refrigerate 30 minutes. Serve zucchini carpaccio sprinkled with 2 tablespoons roasted slivered almonds.
prep time 20 minutes (+ refrigeration) **serves** 8
nutritional count per serving 6g total fat (0.7g saturated fat); 464kJ (111 cal); 12.5g carbohydrate; 1.3g protein; 1.3g fibre

beef carpaccio Tightly wrap 400g piece beef eye fillet in plastic wrap; freeze 1 hour or until firm. Unwrap beef; slice as thinly as possible. Arrange slices on platter. Combine 2 tablespoons olive oil, 2 teaspoons finely grated lemon rind, 2 tablespoons lemon juice, 1 crushed clove garlic, ⅓ cup finely chopped fresh flat-leaf parsley, 2 tablespoons finely chopped fresh oregano and ⅓ cup finely chopped baby rocket leaves in small bowl. Serve beef sprinkled with herb mixture and ⅓ cup flaked parmesan cheese.

prep time 30 minutes (+ freezing) **serves** 8

nutritional count per serving 7.8g total fat (2.3g saturated fat); 506kJ (121 cal); 0.3g carbohydrate; 12.3g protein; 0.3g fibre

kingfish carpaccio Tightly wrap 400g piece sashimi kingfish in plastic wrap; freeze 1 hour or until firm. Unwrap fish; slice as thinly as possible. Arrange slices on platter; drizzle fish with ¼ cup lemon juice. Cover; refrigerate 1 hour. Combine 2 tablespoons olive oil, 1 small red onion, sliced thinly, 1 cup loosely packed fresh flat-leaf parsley leaves and 2 tablespoons rinsed, drained baby capers in medium bowl. Drain juice from fish; serve with onion mixture.

prep time 30 minutes (+ freezing and refrigeration) **serves** 8

nutritional count per serving 5.7g total fat (1g saturated fat); 410kJ (98 cal); 0.9g carbohydrate; 10.5g protein; 0.5g fibre
Use whatever firm white sashimi-type fish you like.

tuna carpaccio Tightly wrap 400g piece sashimi tuna in plastic wrap; freeze 1 hour. Unwrap tuna; slice as thinly as possible. Arrange slices on platter; drizzle tuna with ¼ cup lime juice. Cover; refrigerate 1 hour. Combine 2 tablespoons olive oil, 1 finely chopped fresh long red chilli, ¼ cup finely shredded fresh basil and 2 tablespoons coarsely chopped roasted pistachios in medium bowl. Drain juice from tuna; serve tuna with basil mixture.

prep time 30 minutes (+ freezing and refrigeration) **serves** 8

nutritional count per serving 8.3g total fat (1.9g saturated fat); 535kJ (128 cal); 0.4g carbohydrate; 13g protein; 0.2g fibre

EGGPLANT FRITTERS

2 large eggplants (aubergine) (1kg)
1 cup (100g) coarsely grated mozzarella
  cheese
½ cup coarsely chopped fresh flat-leaf
  parsley
2 cloves garlic, crushed
½ cup (50g) packaged breadcrumbs
¼ cup (35g) plain flour
2 eggs
vegetable oil, for shallow-frying

1 Preheat oven to 220°C/200°C fan-forced.
2 Remove and discard stem ends from
eggplants; prick eggplants all over with fork.
Place on oiled oven tray; roast, uncovered,
about 30 minutes or until soft. Cool. Peel
eggplants; chop flesh finely.
3 Combine eggplant, cheese, parsley, garlic,
breadcrumbs, flour and eggs in large bowl. Using
wetted hands, shape level tablespoons of mixture
into oval patties.
4 Heat oil in large frying pan; cook fritters, in
batches, until browned both sides. Drain on
absorbent paper. Serve fritters warm or cold,
with lemon wedges, if you like.

prep + cook time 1 hour **makes** 36
nutritional count per fritter 5.3g total fat (1g
saturated fat); 272kJ (65 cal); 2.4g carbohydrate;
1.7g protein; 0.8g fibre

PEA AND PANCETTA FRITTATAS

1 teaspoon olive oil
4 slices pancetta (60g), chopped finely
1 clove garlic, crushed
6 eggs
⅔ cup (160ml) cream
½ cup (60g) frozen peas
⅓ cup (25g) finely grated parmesan cheese
1 tablespoon finely chopped fresh mint
1 teaspoon finely grated lemon rind
2 tablespoons crème fraîche
36 small fresh mint leaves

1 Preheat oven to 200°C/180°C fan-forced.
Grease three 12-hole (1-tablespoon/20ml) mini
muffin pans.
2 Heat oil in small frying pan; cook pancetta and
garlic, stirring, until pancetta is crisp. Cool.
3 Whisk eggs and cream in large jug; stir in
pancetta mixture, peas, cheese, mint and rind.
Pour egg mixture into pan holes.
4 Bake frittatas about 12 minutes or until set.
Stand in pan 5 minutes before serving topped with
crème fraîche and mint leaves.

prep + cook time 30 minutes **makes** 36
nutritional count per frittata 3.8g total fat (2.1g
saturated fat); 178kJ (43 cal); 0.4g carbohydrate;
1.9g protein; 0.1g fibre

ricotta-stuffed prosciutto and melon

smoked trout dip

RICOTTA-STUFFED PROSCIUTTO AND MELON

½ medium cantaloupe (850g)
5 slices prosciutto (75g)
150g ricotta cheese
1 tablespoon finely chopped fresh chives
2 tablespoons finely chopped roasted walnuts

1 Peel cantaloupe; cut lengthways into 10 slices.
Cut each slice in half crossways.
2 Cut prosciutto in half lengthways; cut each slice
in half crossways.
3 Combine remaining ingredients in small bowl.
4 Spread cheese mixture over one side of each
prosciutto; wrap prosciutto firmly around melon.

prep time 20 minutes **makes** 20
nutritional count per piece 1.8g total fat (0.7g
saturated fat); 121kJ (29 cal); 1.5g carbohydrate;
1.8g protein; 0.4g fibre
*You could use halved fresh figs instead of the
cantaloupe, if you like.*

SMOKED TROUT DIP

1 medium potato (200g), chopped
  coarsely
¼ cup (60ml) warm milk
150g piece smoked trout, flaked
1 clove garlic, crushed
2 tablespoons olive oil
2 green onions, chopped finely

1 Boil, steam or microwave potato until
tender; drain. Push potato through fine sieve
into small bowl; stir in milk.
2 Combine trout, garlic, oil and onion in
medium bowl; fold in potato mixture.
3 Serve dip with poppy seed crackers,
if you like.

prep + cook time 30 minutes
makes 1½ cups
nutritional count per teaspoon 0.7g total
fat (0.1g saturated fat); 46kJ (11 cal); 0.4g
carbohydrate; 0.7g protein; 0.1g fibre

ROASTED VEGETABLE AND MASCARPONE TERRINE

1 medium red capsicum (bell pepper) (200g)

1 medium zucchini (courgette) (120g), sliced thinly lengthways

2 baby eggplants (aubergine) (120g), sliced thinly lengthways

12 slices prosciutto (180g)

250g mascarpone cheese

2 eggs

¼ cup finely chopped fresh basil

1 Preheat oven to 200°C/180°C fan-forced.

2 Quarter capsicums; discard seeds and membranes. Roast, skin-side up, until skin blisters and blackens. Cover capsicum with plastic or paper for 5 minutes; peel away skin, then chop capsicum finely.

3 Meanwhile, cook zucchini and eggplant, in batches, on heated oiled grill plate until tender; cool. Chop vegetables finely.

4 Reduce oven temperature to 180°C/160°C fan-forced. Grease 8cm x 26cm bar pan.

5 Line base and sides of pan with prosciutto, leaving 7cm overhang on sides of pan.

6 Combine cheese and eggs in medium bowl; stir in vegetables and basil. Carefully spread mixture into pan; fold prosciutto over to cover mixture. Cover pan tightly with foil; place on oven tray.

7 Roast terrine 30 minutes. Uncover, roast 30 minutes or until terrine is firm. Cool. Refrigerate terrine 3 hours before cutting into 16 slices.

prep + cook time 1 hour 30 minutes (+ refrigeration) **makes** 16 slices
nutritional count per slice 14.9g total fat (9.4g saturated fat); 702kJ (168 cal); 1.9g carbohydrate; 6.7g protein; 0.7g fibre

CHEESE AND SPINACH POLENTA

1 litre (4 cups) milk
1 cup (170g) polenta
½ cup (50g) coarsely grated mozzarella
cheese
¼ cup (20g) finely grated parmesan cheese
250g finely chopped thawed, drained frozen
spinach
250g vine-ripened cherry tomatoes, halved
1 tablespoon balsamic vinegar
1 tablespoon olive oil

1 Grease 20cm x 30cm lamington pan.
2 Bring milk to the boil in medium saucepan;
gradually stir in polenta. Cook, stirring, about 10
minutes or until polenta thickens. Stir in cheeses
and spinach. Spread polenta mixture into pan,
cover; refrigerate 2 hours or overnight or until firm.
3 Preheat oven to 200°C/180°C fan-forced.
4 Turn polenta onto board; cut into 30 squares.
Place polenta onto baking-paper-lined oven tray.
Bake about 20 minutes or until browned lightly.
5 Meanwhile, combine tomato, vinegar and oil in
small baking dish. Roast, alongside polenta, about
15 minutes or until tomato softens slightly.
6 Serve polenta squares topped with tomato
halves; drizzle with tomato pan juices.

prep + cook time 45 minutes (+ refrigeration)
makes 30
nutritional count per piece 2.6g total fat (1.3g
saturated fat); 242kJ (58 cal); 5.7g carbohydrate;
2.5g protein; 0.5g fibre

FRIED BOCCONCINI WITH CAPSICUM SAUCE

1 medium red capsicum (bell pepper) (200g)
2 medium egg tomatoes (150g), halved
2 cloves garlic, unpeeled
2 teaspoons olive oil
2 tablespoons plain flour
1 egg, beaten lightly
½ cup (50g) breadcrumbs
¼ cup (20g) finely grated parmesan cheese
2 tablespoons finely chopped fresh
    flat-leaf parsley
2 teaspoons finely grated lemon rind
16 cherry bocconcini (mini mozzarella balls)
    (240g)
vegetable oil, for deep-frying

1 Preheat oven to 220°C/200°C fan-forced.
2 Quarter capsicum; remove seeds and membranes. Combine capsicum, tomato, garlic and oil in small baking dish; roast, uncovered, about 20 minutes or until vegetables soften.
3 Peel garlic; blend or process garlic and vegetable mixture until smooth.
4 Place flour and egg in separate small shallow bowls. Combine breadcrumbs, parmesan, parsley and rind in another small shallow bowl.
5 Coat bocconcini in flour; shake off excess. Dip in egg, then in breadcrumb mixture.
6 Meanwhile heat oil in wok; deep-fry bocconcini, in batches, until golden. Drain on wire rack over tray.
7 Serve bocconcini with roasted capsicum sauce.

prep + cook time 1 hour makes 16
nutritional count per cheese ball 4.5g total fat (2.1g saturated fat); 309kJ (74 cal); 3.8g carbohydrate; 4.3g protein; 0.5g fibre

BARBECUED SEAFOOD PLATTER

16 uncooked medium king prawns (720g)
1 teaspoon finely grated lemon rind
½ teaspoon dried chilli flakes
1 clove garlic, crushed
1 tablespoon finely chopped fresh oregano
2 tablespoons olive oil
8 slices prosciutto (120g)
8 butterflied sardines (240g)
300g baby octopus, quartered
200g squid hoods, sliced into rings
2 tablespoons balsamic vinegar
¼ cup coarsely chopped fresh flat-leaf
    parsley
500g small black mussels
¼ cup (60ml) lemon juice
1 medium tomato (150g), seeded, chopped
    finely

1 Remove and discard prawn heads. Cut prawns lengthwise, three-quarters of the way through, (and down to 1cm before the tail) leaving shells intact; press down on prawns on board to flatten.

2 Combine prawns, rind, chilli, garlic, oregano and half the oil in medium bowl; cover, refrigerate 1 hour.

3 Wrap a prosciutto slice firmly around each sardine.

4 Cook octopus and squid on heated oiled grill plate (or grill or barbecue). Combine octopus and squid in medium heatproof bowl with remaining oil, vinegar and 2 tablespoons of the parsley. Cover to keep warm.

5 Cook prawns and sardines on heated oiled grill plate (or grill or barbecue).

6 Meanwhile, cook mussels, covered, on heated oiled flat plate about 5 minutes or until mussels open (discard any that do not). Place mussels in medium heatproof bowl; drizzle with juice, sprinkle with tomato and remaining parsley. Serve seafood with lemon wedges, if you like.

prep + cook time 1 hour (+ refrigeration)
serves 8
nutritional count per serving 8.7g total fat (1.7g saturated fat); 836kJ (200 cal); 1.3g carbohydrate; 28.5g protein; 0.4g fibre

BITES & SPREADS

goats cheese and chive pastries Preheat oven to 200°C/180°C fan-forced. Combine 240g soft goats cheese, ¼ cup finely chopped fresh chives, ¼ cup finely chopped roasted slivered almonds and ¼ cup finely chopped seeded prunes in small bowl. Spray one of 16 filo sheets with cooking-oil spray. Top with another pastry sheet. Repeat to make four stacks. Cut each stack into four to make 16 rectangles. Place level tablespoons of cheese mixture along short sides of each rectangle. Roll pastry once over filling; fold in both sides then roll up to form cigars. Place pastries on lined oven tray; bake 15 minutes.

prep + cook time 1 hour
makes 16
nutritional count per pastry
3.6g total fat (1.7g saturated fat); 351kJ (84 cal); 8.8g carbohydrate; 3.7g protein; 0.7g fibre

blue cheese toasts with pear and watercress Preheat grill. Cut 1 small french bread stick into 1cm slices. Brush bread both sides with combined 40g melted butter and 1 clove crushed garlic; place bread, in single layer, on oven tray. Toast bread both sides. Thinly slice 1 medium pear. Spread toasts with 200g soft blue cheese; top with pear slices and 1 cup trimmed watercress.

prep + cook time 30 minutes
makes 20
nutritional count per piece
5.2g total fat (3.2g saturated fat); 334kJ (80 cal); 5.2g carbohydrate; 2.8g protein; 0.7g fibre

fig and quince paste Peel, core and quarter 1kg quinces; combine in large saucepan with 1 cup chopped dried figs, 1 cinnamon stick and enough water to cover, bring to the boil. Simmer, covered, about 1 hour or until most liquid is absorbed. Discard cinnamon; process mixture until pulpy. Measure mixture into same pan. Add 1 cup caster sugar to every 1 cup pulp; stir in ¼ cup lemon juice, stir until sugar dissolves. Cook, over very low heat, 2 hours or until mixture leaves side of pan. Pour into oiled and lined deep 20cm-round cake pan. Stand at room temperature overnight until set. Serve as part of a cheese platter.

prep + cook time 3½ hours (+ standing) **makes** 4 cups
nutritional count per teaspoon
0g total fat (0g saturated fat); 79kJ (19 cal); 4.5g carbohydrate; 0.1g protein; 0.4g fibre

blue cheese and caramelised onion dip Melt 20g butter in medium saucepan; cook 1 coarsely chopped large brown onion, stirring, until onion softens. Add 2 tablespoons brown sugar and 2 tablespoons white wine vinegar; cook, stirring, over low heat, about 10 minutes or until onion is caramelised. Stir in 100g crumbled blue cheese and ¾ cup crème fraîche until smooth. Cool. Cover; refrigerate until cold. Stir in ¼ cup finely chopped fresh flat-leaf parsley.

prep + cook time 30 minutes
makes 1½ cups
nutritional count per teaspoon
1.7g total fat (1.1g saturated fat); 84kJ (20 cal); 0.7g carbohydrate; 0.4g protein; 0.1g fibre

baked brie Preheat oven to 200°C/180°C fan-forced. Grease 1 cup ovenproof dish (10cm diameter, 4cm deep.) Place whole 200g brie in dish. Make six small slits into cheese. Cut 1 sprig fresh thyme into six pieces; push thyme into slits. Pour 2 tablespoons dry red wine over cheese; cover dish, place on oven tray. Bake 20 minutes. Stand, covered, 5 minutes. Sprinkle with 1 teaspoon finely grated lemon rind and 1 finely chopped fresh thyme sprig to serve.

prep + cook time 40 minutes
serves 8
nutritional count per serving
7.3g total fat (4.7g saturated fat); 368kJ (88 cal); 0g carbohydrate; 4.8g protein; 0g fibre

FRIED CAULIFLOWER

1 small cauliflower (1kg), cut into florets

3 eggs

½ cup (125ml) milk

½ cup (75g) self-raising flour

¼ cup (20g) finely grated parmesan cheese

2 tablespoons finely chopped fresh flat-leaf parsley

vegetable oil, for deep-frying

1 Boil, steam or microwave cauliflower until tender; drain. Cool.

2 Whisk eggs, milk, flour, cheese and parsley in medium shallow bowl until smooth.

3 Heat oil in wok. Dip cauliflower into batter; drain off excess. Deep-fry cauliflower, in batches, until browned lightly. Drain on absorbent paper.

4 Serve cauliflower with lemon wedges, if you like.

prep + cook time 40 minutes **serves** 16
nutritional count per serving 4.6g total fat (1.1g saturated fat); 326kJ (78 cal); 4.9g carbohydrate; 3.7g protein; 1.2g fibre

MARINATED MUSHROOMS

1 litre (4 cups) white vinegar
1 cup (250ml) dry white wine
1 tablespoon sea salt flakes
800g button mushrooms, halved
2 cloves garlic, sliced thinly
½ teaspoon dried chilli flakes
1 tablespoon coarsely chopped fresh
   rosemary
1 tablespoon finely chopped fresh
   flat-leaf parsley
3 x 5cm strips lemon rind
1 bay leaf
2 cups (500ml) olive oil

1 Sterilise 1-litre (4-cup) jar and lid.
2 Combine vinegar, wine and half the salt
in medium saucepan; heat without boiling.
Add mushrooms; simmer, uncovered, about
5 minutes or until tender. Drain mushrooms;
discard liquid.
3 Combine hot mushrooms, garlic, chilli,
herbs, rind, bay leaf and remaining salt in large
heatproof bowl. Spoon mushroom mixture into
hot sterilised jar.
4 Heat oil in small saucepan; carefully pour over
mushrooms in jar to completely cover mushrooms,
leaving a 1cm space between mushrooms and
top of jar. Seal while hot.

prep + cook time 40 minutes **makes** 4 cups
nutritional count per ¼ cup 28.6g total fat
(4g saturated fat); 1145kJ (274 cal); 0.2g
carbohydrate; 1.9g protein; 1.3g fibre
Store marinated mushrooms in refrigerator for up to
three months. Serve mushrooms with crusty bread
or as part of an antipasto platter with cheeses and
deli meats.

veal braciole

arancini

VEAL BRACIOLE

⅔ cup (45g) stale breadcrumbs
1 tablespoon rinsed drained baby capers,
   chopped finely
2 cloves garlic, crushed
5 veal schnitzels (500g) (see note, below)
1 medium lemon (140g), quartered, sliced
   thickly
20 fresh bay leaves
1 tablespoon olive oil

1 Combine breadcrumbs, capers and garlic in small bowl.
2 Using meat mallet, gently pound veal, one piece at a time, between sheets of plastic wrap until 5mm thick; cut each piece in half crossways.
3 Press 1 level tablespoon of crumb mixture over one side of each piece of veal. Roll veal up tightly; cut each roll in half.
4 Thread lemon slices, veal rolls and bay leaves onto 20 small bamboo skewers or strong toothpicks. Brush skewers all over with oil; cook on heated oiled grill plate (or grill or barbecue) until veal is cooked through.

prep + cook time 40 minutes **makes** 20
nutritional count per piece 1.4g total fat (0.2g saturated fat); 184kJ (44 cal); 1.7g carbohydrate; 5.9g protein; 0.3g fibre
We used plain uncrumbed schnitzel, sometimes called escalopes, in this recipe.
You need 20 small bamboo skewers or strong toothpicks for this recipe. Soak skewers in cold water at least an hour before using to prevent them scorching during cooking.

ARANCINI

2 cups (500ml) chicken stock
½ cup (125ml) dry white wine
40g butter
1 small brown onion (80g), chopped finely
1 clove garlic, crushed
1 cup (200g) arborio rice
⅓ cup (25g) finely grated parmesan cheese
⅓ cup (35g) coarsely grated mozzarella
   cheese
24 feta-stuffed green olives (240g)
⅓ cup (35g) packaged breadcrumbs
vegetable oil, for deep-frying

1 Combine stock and wine in medium saucepan; bring to the boil. Reduce heat; simmer, covered.
2 Meanwhile, melt butter in medium saucepan; cook onion and garlic, stirring, until onion softens. Add rice; stir over medium heat until rice is coated in butter mixture. Stir in ½ cup of the simmering stock mixture; cook, stirring, over low heat until liquid is absorbed. Continue adding mixture, in ½ cup batches, stirring, until liquid is absorbed after each addition. Total cooking time should be about 35 minutes or until rice is tender. Stir in cheeses, cover; cool 30 minutes.
3 Roll rounded tablespoons of risotto mixture into balls; press an olive into centre of each ball, roll to enclose. Coat risotto balls in breadcrumbs.
4 Heat oil in wok; deep-fry risotto balls, in batches, until browned lightly. Drain on absorbent paper.

prep + cook time 1 hour 30 minutes (+ cooling)
makes 24
nutritional count per ball 5.7g total fat (1.8g saturated fat); 401kJ (96 cal); 8.1g carbohydrate; 1.9g protein; 1g fibre

RISOTTO-FILLED ZUCCHINI FLOWERS

2 cups (500ml) chicken stock
½ cup (125ml) dry white wine
pinch saffron
40g butter
1 small brown onion (80g), chopped finely
1 clove garlic, crushed
1 cup (200g) arborio rice
⅓ cup (25g) finely grated parmesan cheese
1 teaspoon finely grated lemon rind
2 tablespoons finely chopped
   fresh flat-leaf parsley
28 zucchini flowers with stem attached
   (420g)
cooking-oil spray

1 Combine stock, wine and saffron in medium saucepan; bring to the boil. Reduce heat; simmer, covered.
2 Meanwhile, melt butter in medium saucepan; cook onion and garlic, stirring, until onion softens. Add rice; stir over medium heat until rice is coated in butter mixture. Stir in ½ cup of the simmering stock mixture; cook, stirring, over low heat until liquid is absorbed. Continue adding stock mixture, in ½ cup batches, stirring, until liquid is absorbed after each addition. Total cooking time should be about 35 minutes or until rice is tender. Stir in cheese, rind and parsley, cover; cool 30 minutes.
3 Preheat oven to 200°C/180°C fan-forced. Grease two oven trays.
4 Discard stamens from zucchini flowers; fill flowers with 1 level tablespoon of risotto mixture, twist petal tops to enclose filling.
5 Place zucchini flowers on trays; spray all over with cooking-oil spray. Roast, uncovered, about 15 minutes or until zucchini stems are tender.

prep + cook time 1 hour 30 minutes
(+ cooking) **makes** 28
nutritional count per flower 1.8g total fat
(1g saturated fat); 209kJ (50 cal); 6.2g
carbohydrate; 1.3g protein; 0.4g fibre
If you don't want to make 28 zucchini flowers
– just eat the delicious risotto as it is.

TOMATO TARTS

4 medium vine-ripened tomatoes (600g),
   peeled, quartered, seeded
1 tablespoon brown sugar
1 tablespoon balsamic vinegar
½ sheet ready-rolled puff pastry
16 sprigs fresh chervil

1 Preheat oven 220°C/200°C fan-forced.
2 Combine tomato, sugar and vinegar in small baking dish; roast, uncovered, about 20 minutes or until tomato is soft.
3 Meanwhile, cut pastry sheet in half lengthways, cut each half into 4 squares; cut each square into triangles (you will have 16). Place pastry triangles on oiled oven tray; top with another oiled oven tray (the second tray stops the pastry from puffing up). Bake pastry, alongside tomato, about 10 minutes or until crisp.
4 Place a tomato piece on each pastry triangle. Serve topped with chervil.

prep + cook time 40 minutes **makes** 16
nutritional count per tart 1.2g total fat (0.6g saturated fat); 117kJ (28 cal); 3.4g carbohydrate; 0.7g protein; 0.5g fibre

SWEET AND SOUR BEETROOT

2 large beetroot (400g), peeled, grated
   coarsely
3 green onions, sliced thinly
1 tablespoon finely chopped fresh dill
2 tablespoons red wine vinegar
1 tablespoon olive oil
1 teaspoon wholegrain mustard
2 teaspoons caster sugar
1 red endive (125g), leaves separated
   (see note)

1 Combine beetroot, onion, dill, vinegar, oil,
mustard and sugar in medium bowl.
2 Serve beetroot mixture with endive leaves.

prep time 15 minutes **makes** 24
nutritional count per piece 0.8g total fat
(0.1g saturated fat); 71kJ (17 cal); 1.7g
carbohydrate; 0.4g protein; 0.6g fibre
You need 24 endive leaves for this recipe.

MEATBALLS NAPOLITANA

500g beef mince
1 egg
½ cup (50g) breadcrumbs
¼ cup (20g) finely grated parmesan cheese
¼ cup finely chopped fresh flat-leaf parsley
2 tablespoons olive oil
1 small brown onion (80g), chopped finely
1 clove garlic, crushed
700g bottled tomato pasta sauce
½ cup (60g) frozen peas
¼ cup coarsely chopped fresh basil

1 Combine mince, egg, breadcrumbs, cheese and parsley in medium bowl. Using wetted hands, roll level tablespoons of mince mixture into balls.
2 Heat half the oil in large frying pan; cook meatballs, in batches, until browned and cooked through.
3 Heat remaining oil in same pan; cook onion and garlic, stirring, until onion softens. Add sauce; bring to the boil. Add meatballs, reduce heat; simmer, uncovered, about 10 minutes or until sauce thickens slightly. Add peas and basil; simmer, uncovered, until peas are tender.
4 Serve meatballs and sauce with crusty bread, if you like.

prep + cook time 1 hour **makes** 26
nutritional count per meatball 3.9g total fat (1.2g saturated fat); 305kJ (73 cal); 4.1g carbohydrate; 4.9g protein; 0.8g fibre

FISH AND CAPER CROQUETTES

¾ cup (180ml) water
¾ cup (180ml) dry white wine
2 bay leaves
400g skinless boneless firm white
   fish fillets
40g butter
¼ cup (35g) plain flour
1 cup (250ml) milk
2 teaspoons finely grated lemon rind
2 tablespoons rinsed drained baby
   capers, chopped finely
1 clove garlic, crushed
1 tablespoon finely chopped fresh chives
¼ cup (35g) plain flour, extra
1 egg, beaten lightly
1 cup (70g) stale breadcrumbs
vegetable oil, for shallow-frying
1 medium lemon, sliced thickly

1 Combine the water, wine and bay leaves in small saucepan; bring to the boil. Add fish, reduce heat; simmer, covered, about 5 minutes or until fish is cooked through. Drain fish; discard cooking liquid, flake fish coarsely.
2 Meanwhile, melt butter in medium saucepan. Add flour; cook, stirring, about 2 minutes or until mixture thickens and bubbles. Gradually stir in milk; cook, stirring, until mixture boils and thickens. Remove from heat; stir in rind, capers, garlic, chives and fish. Cover; refrigerate 2 hours.
3 Roll rounded tablespoons of fish mixture into ovals; coat in extra flour, shake off excess. Dip croquettes in egg then breadcrumbs.
4 Heat oil in large frying pan; cook croquettes until browned all over. Drain on absorbent paper. Serve with lemon slices.

prep + cook time 40 minutes (+ refrigeration)
makes 16
nutritional count per croquette 7.9g total fat (2.6g saturated fat); 573kJ (137 cal); 7.2g carbohydrate; 7.2g protein; 0.6g fibre

MEZZE

CHICKEN, SPINACH AND CHEESE GÖZLEME

2 cups (300g) plain flour
½ teaspoon salt
¾ cup (180ml) warm water
2 tablespoons olive oil
1 medium brown onion (150g),
   chopped finely
2 cloves garlic, crushed
2 teaspoons ground cumin
1 teaspoon ground cinnamon
200g spinach, trimmed
1 cup finely shredded cooked chicken
100g feta cheese, crumbled
2 tablespoons lemon juice

1 Combine flour and salt in medium bowl. Gradually stir in the water; mix to a soft dough. Knead dough on floured surface about 5 minutes or until smooth and elastic. Return to bowl; cover, while preparing filling.

2 Heat half the oil in medium frying pan; cook onion and garlic, stirring, until onion softens. Add spices; cook, stirring, until fragrant. Transfer mixture to medium heatproof bowl; cool.

3 Meanwhile, boil, steam or microwave spinach until wilted; rinse under cold water, drain. Squeeze out excess water; shred spinach finely. Stir spinach, chicken, cheese and juice into onion mixture.

4 Divide dough in half; roll each piece on floured surface into 25cm x 35cm rectangle. Divide spinach filling across centre of each rectangle. Fold top and bottom edges of dough over filling; tuck in ends to enclose.

5 Cook gözleme, both sides, on heated oiled grill plate (or grill or barbecue), over low heat, brushing with remaining oil until browned lightly and heated through. Stand 5 minutes before cutting each gözleme into 8 slices; serve with lemon wedges, if you like.

prep + cook time 1 hour 30 minutes
makes 16
nutritional count per slice 4.6g total fat (1.5g saturated fat); 514kJ (123 cal); 14.2g carbohydrate; 5.5g protein; 1.1g fibre

FRIED FISH SANDWICHES

2 cloves garlic, unpeeled
½ cup (140g) greek-style yogurt
¼ cup finely chopped fresh mint
8 small white fish fillets (320g), skin on
2 tablespoons plain flour
2 teaspoons smoked paprika
1 teaspoon ground cumin
1 tablespoon olive oil
1 loaf turkish bread (430g), split, toasted
1 baby cos lettuce, leaves separated
2 medium tomatoes (300g), sliced thinly
½ small red onion (50g), sliced thinly

1 Preheat oven to 200°C/180°C fan-forced.
2 Place garlic on oven tray; roast, uncovered, about 10 minutes or until soft. Cool; peel garlic.
3 Blend or process garlic and yogurt until smooth; stir in mint.
4 Coat fish in combined flour and spices; shake off excess. Heat oil in large frying pan; cook fish, both sides, until browned and crisp.
5 Spread yogurt over one half of bread; top with lettuce, tomato, onion, fish and remaining bread. Cut into 12 slices.

prep + cook time 30 minutes **makes** 12
nutritional count per slice 4.2g total fat (1.1g saturated fat); 673kJ (161 cal); 19.5g carbohydrate; 10.1g protein; 1.8g fibre
We used sand whiting fillets in this recipe.

BARBECUED BABY OCTOPUS

1kg baby octopus
⅓ cup (80ml) lemon juice
⅓ cup (80ml) olive oil
2 cloves garlic, crushed
2 teaspoons dried oregano
1 medium lemon, cut into wedges

1 Clean octopus; remove eyes and beaks.
Combine octopus with juice, oil, garlic and dried
oregano in medium bowl. Cover, refrigerate 3 hours
or overnight.
2 Drain octopus; discard marinade. Cook octopus
on heated oiled barbecue (or grill or grill plate) until
tender. Serve with lemon wedges.

prep + cook time 25 minutes (+ refrigeration)
serves 6 **nutritional count per serving** 13.4g
total fat (1.7g saturated fat); 982kJ (235 cal);
1g carbohydrate; 27.6g protein; 0.2g fibre
*Dried oregano is a type of wild oregano.
It has a stronger flavour than regular oregano
and is used in many Greek dishes.
You can find dried oregano at specialty
supermarkets and delicatessens.
If unavailable, use dried oregano.
Octopus is best cooked just before serving.*

RADISH AND HERB SALAD

2 large pitta breads (160g), cut into wedges

1 medium green capsicum (bell pepper) (200g), chopped finely

1 lebanese cucumber (130g), seeded, chopped finely

1 medium tomato (150g), chopped finely

4 red radishes (140g), grated coarsely

½ cup finely chopped fresh flat-leaf parsley

⅓ cup finely chopped fresh mint

¼ cup coarsely chopped fresh coriander

2 tablespoons olive oil

2 tablespoons lemon juice

2 cloves garlic, crushed

1 Preheat grill.

2 Place bread on oven trays; grill about 5 minutes or until browned both sides and crisp.

3 Combine remaining ingredients in medium bowl. Serve salad with pitta crisps.

prep + cook time 25 minutes **serves** 8
nutritional count per serving 5.2g total fat (0.7g saturated fat); 468kJ (112 cal); 12.6g carbohydrate; 2.8g protein; 1.9g fibre

20

SPICY TUNISIAN TUNA SALAD

2 teaspoons caraway seeds
½ teaspoon ground cinnamon
425g can tuna in oil
300g can chickpeas, rinsed, drained
1 small green capsicum (bell pepper)
  (150g), cut into 1cm pieces
⅓ cup (40g) seeded black olives,
  chopped coarsely
200g cherry tomatoes, quartered
2 green onions, sliced thinly
2 teaspoons finely grated orange rind
2 tablespoons orange juice
1 tablespoon harissa

1 Dry-fry spices in small frying pan until
fragrant; cool.
2 Drain tuna; reserve 2 tablespoons of the oil.
Flake tuna coarsely.
3 Combine tuna, reserved oil, spices and
remaining ingredients in large bowl. Serve with
toasted turkish bread.

prep + cook time 25 minutes serves 8
nutritional count per serving 12g total fat
(1.8g saturated fat); 782kJ (187 cal); 6.2g
carbohydrate; 12.7g protein; 2.1g fibre

PICKLED OCTOPUS

1.5kg large octopus
¾ cup (180ml) extra virgin olive oil
½ cup (125ml) white wine vinegar
1 clove garlic, crushed
2 tablespoons coarsely chopped
    fresh flat-leaf parsley

1 Clean octopus, remove eyes and beak. Place octopus in large saucepan without any liquid. Cover pan, cook over low heat about 1 hour or until octopus is tender. (The octopus will cook in its own juices but, if necessary, add a little water if the juices evaporate.) Cool octopus in pan until it is cool enough to handle. Rinse octopus under cold water, remove skin, leaving tentacles intact.
2 Cut octopus into bite-size pieces; combine in medium bowl with remaining ingredients. Cover, refrigerate overnight. Serve sprinkled with parsley; accompany with lemon wedges, if you like.

prep + cook time 1 hour 10 minutes (+ cooling and refrigeration) **serves** 8
nutritional count per serving 21.8g total fat (2.9g saturated fat); 1333kJ (319 cal); 0.2g carbohydrate; 30.8g protein; 0.1g fibre
We used large octopus in this recipe, but you could also use baby octopus. Recipe can be made up to four days ahead; store, covered, in the refrigerator.

BLOOD ORANGE AND CHILLI GLAZED QUAIL

6 quails (960g)
1 teaspoon cumin seeds
½ cup (125ml) blood orange juice
1 fresh long red chilli, chopped finely
1 clove garlic, crushed
2 tablespoons brown sugar
1 tablespoon finely chopped fresh coriander

1 Using kitchen scissors, cut along both sides of quails' backbones; discard backbones. Halve each quail along breastbone; cut each in half again to give a total of 24 pieces.
2 Cook quail, covered, on heated oiled grill plate (or grill or barbecue) about 20 minutes or until cooked through.
3 Meanwhile, dry-fry seeds in small saucepan until fragrant. Add juice, chilli, garlic and sugar; stir over heat, without boiling, until sugar dissolves. Bring to the boil; boil, uncovered, about 5 minutes or until mixture is thick and syrupy.
4 Combine hot quail, syrup and coriander in large bowl.

prep + cook time 35 minutes **serves** 8
nutritional count per serving 6.6g total fat (1.7g saturated fat); 514kJ (123 cal); 4.4g carbohydrate; 11.3g protein; 0.1g fibre
Quails are available from specialist food stores and most poultry shops.

LEMON PEPPER SQUID

500g squid hoods
½ cup (75g) plain flour
2 tablespoons lemon pepper
2 teaspoons dried oregano
1 teaspoon coarse cooking salt
peanut oil, for deep-frying
1 tablespoon coarsely chopped fresh
  parsley

1 Cut squid down centre to open out; score inside
in diagonal pattern then cut into thick strips.
2 Combine flour, lemon pepper, dried oregano and salt
in large bowl; add squid, toss to coat in mixture, shake away excess.
3 Heat oil in medium saucepan; deep-fry squid, in batches, until tender. Drain on absorbent paper. Serve sprinkled with parsley.

prep + cook time 30 minutes **serves** 4
nutritional count per serving 8.1g total fat (1.7g saturated fat); 953kJ (228 cal); 14.4g carbohydrate; 23.3g protein; 1.7g fibre
Lemon pepper is a blend of crushed black pepper, lemon, herbs and spices. It's available from the dried herb and spice section at most supermarkets. If you use one containing salt, reduce the salt quantity in this recipe.
Dried oregano is a type of wild oregano. It has a stronger flavour than regular oregano and is used in many Greek dishes. You can find dried oregano at specialty supermarkets and delicatessens. If unavailable, use dried oregano.

 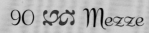

blood orange and chilli glazed quail

lemon pepper squid

TURKISH TOMATO SALAD

1 teaspoon cumin seeds

2 medium tomatoes (300g), chopped finely

1 medium red capsicum (bell pepper) (200g), chopped finely

1 small red onion (100g), chopped finely

1 fresh long red chilli, chopped finely

¼ cup finely chopped fresh flat-leaf parsley

1 tablespoon pomegranate molasses

2 tablespoons olive oil

1 Dry-fry seeds in small frying pan until fragrant; cool.

2 Combine seeds with remaining ingredients in medium bowl. Serve with toasted turkish bread.

prep + cook time 20 minutes **serves** 8
nutritional count per serving 4.6g total fat (0.6g saturated fat); 234kJ (56 cal); 2.3g carbohydrate; 0.9g protein; 1g fibre

GRILLED HALOUMI

500g haloumi cheese
2 tablespoons lemon juice
1 tablespoon coarsely chopped
  fresh flat-leaf parsley

1 Cut cheese into 1cm slices. Cook cheese on heated oiled flat plate until browned both sides.
2 Transfer cheese to serving plate; drizzle with juice. Serve immediately, sprinkled with parsley.

prep + cook time 10 minutes **serves** 6
nutritional count per serving 14.3g total fat
(9.2g saturated fat); 861kJ (206 cal); 1.7g
carbohydrate; 17.8g protein; 0g fibre
*Haloumi is best cooked just before serving as it
becomes tough and rubbery on cooling.*

 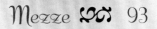

CHEESE PASTRIES

1½ cups (225g) plain flour
1½ cups (225g) self-raising flour
½ teaspoon salt
¾ cup (180ml) warm water
¼ cup (60ml) olive oil
1 egg, beaten lightly
2 teaspoons sesame seeds
filling
1 egg, beaten lightly
100g feta cheese, crumbled
½ cup (120g) ricotta cheese
½ cup (40g) finely grated romano cheese

1 Preheat oven to 200°C/180°C fan-forced. Oil oven trays; line with baking paper.
2 Process flours and salt until combined. While motor is operating, add enough of the combined water and oil so the mixture forms a ball (do not overmix). Remove dough from bowl, wrap in plastic; cover, refrigerate 30 minutes.
3 Meanwhile, make filling.
4 Divide dough in half. Roll each half on floured surface to 30cm x 40cm rectangle; cut 13 x 8.5cm rounds from dough. Drop rounded teaspoons of filling onto rounds; brush edges with a little water. Fold rounds in half, press edges together with a fork to seal. Place pastries on trays; brush with egg, sprinkle with seeds. Bake about 15 minutes or until browned lightly. filling Combine ingredients in medium bowl.

prep + cook time 1 hour 15 minutes (+ refrigeration) **makes** 26 nutritional **count per pastry** 4.7g total fat (1.6g saturated fat); 456kJ (109 cal); 12.4g carbohydrate; 4g protein; 0.7g fibre

Parmesan cheese can be used instead of romano cheese. Pastries can be served warm or cold. Uncooked pastries are suitable to freeze. It is best to cut pastry into the 26 rounds from the first rolling of pastry, as the pastry is not suitable to reroll.

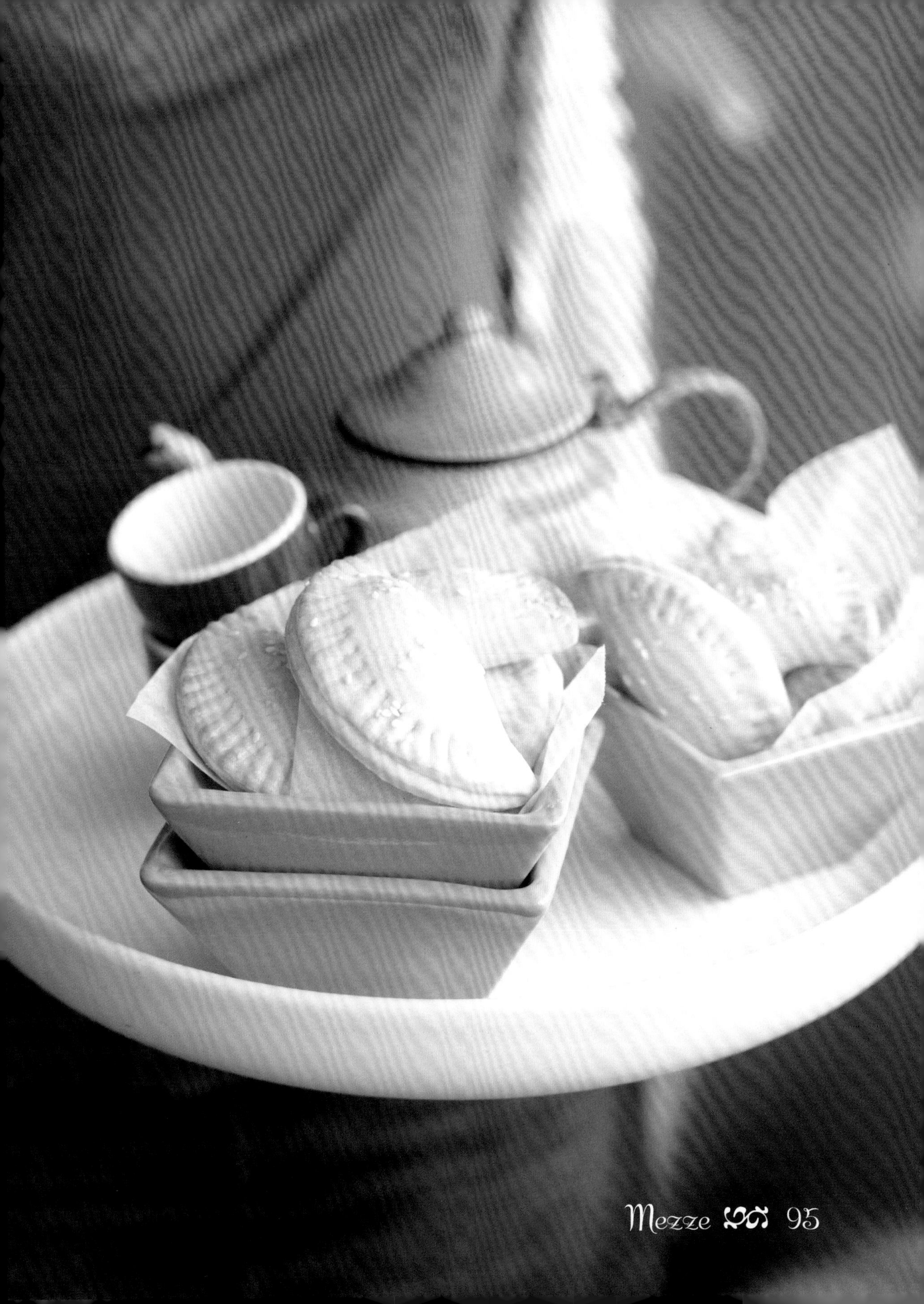

Soak skewers in water for at least an hour prior to using to prevent them from scorching during cooking.

SKEWERS

lemon, garlic and oregano lamb skewers Cut 800g lamb fillets into 2cm pieces. Combine lamb in medium bowl with 1 tablespoon olive oil, 2 teaspoons finely grated lemon rind, 1 clove crushed garlic and 2 tablespoons finely chopped fresh oregano. Cover; refrigerate 1 hour. Stir in 1 tablespoon lemon juice. Thread lamb onto 16 small bamboo skewers or strong toothpicks; cook on heated oiled grill plate (or grill or barbecue) until cooked through.
prep + cook time 30 minutes (+ refrigeration) **makes** 16
nutritional count per skewer 2.9g total fat (1g saturated fat); 284kJ (68 cal); 0g carbohydrate; 10.3g protein; 0g fibre

sumac and sesame chicken skewers Cut 600g chicken breast fillets into 2cm cubes; thread onto 16 small bamboo skewers or strong toothpicks. Combine 1 tablespoon sumac, 1 teaspoon sesame seeds and 1 teaspoon black sesame seeds in small bowl; sprinkle sumac mixture all over skewers. Cook skewers on heated oiled grill plate (or grill or barbecue) until chicken is cooked through. Serve with lemon wedges.
prep + cook time 30 minutes **makes** 16
nutritional count per skewer 2.6g total fat (0.7g saturated fat); 222kJ (53 cal); 0g carbohydrate; 8.1g protein; 0g fibre
Sumac is a purple-red, astringent spice ground from wild Mediterranean berries; it adds a tart, lemony flavour.

vegetable and haloumi
skewers Cut 180g haloumi
cheese into sixteen 2cm cubes;
cut 1 small red capsicum (bell
pepper) into 2cm pieces. Cut 1
large zucchini (courgette) in half
lengthways; cut each half into
eight 2cm pieces. Thread
haloumi, capsicum and zucchini
onto 16 small bamboo skewers
or strong toothpicks; cook on
heated oiled grill plate (or grill or
barbecue) until tender. Meanwhile,
combine ½ cup mayonnaise,
1 tablespoon lime juice and 2
teaspoons harissa in small bowl.
Serve skewers with mayonnaise.
prep + cook time 35 minutes
makes 16
nutritional count per skewer
26.2g total fat (4g saturated fat);
1296kJ (310 cal); 15.6g
carbohydrate; 3.4g protein;
0.7g fibre

lamb kebabs with yogurt and
pitta bread Combine 500g lamb
mince, 1 egg, 1 finely chopped
small brown onion, 2 tablespoons
finely chopped fresh flat-leaf
parsley, 1 crushed clove garlic,
2 teaspoons each ground
cinnamon and sweet paprika and
½ teaspoon cayenne pepper in
bowl. Form lamb mixture into 16
sausage shapes, thread onto
16 small bamboo skewers or
strong toothpicks; flatten slightly.
Cook on heated oiled grill plate
(or grill or barbecue) until browned
and cooked as desired. Serve
kebabs with ½ cup yogurt, lemon
wedges and pitta bread.
prep + cook time 30 minutes
serves 4 (makes 16 skewers)
nutritional count per serving
10.8g total fat (4.8g saturated fat);
1004kJ (240 cal); 5.6g
carbohydrate; 29.2g protein;
0.4g fibre

chermoulla prawn skewers
Shell and devein 16 uncooked
medium king prawns, leaving tails
intact. Combine prawns with 1
tablespoon olive oil, 2 tablespoons
each finely chopped fresh flat-leaf
parsley, mint and coriander, 2
cloves crushed garlic, 2 teaspoons
finely grated lemon rind, 1
tablespoon lemon juice, 1 teaspoon
ground allspice and 1 teaspoon
caraway seeds in medium bowl.
Preheat grill. Thread prawns, tail-
end first, onto 16 small bamboo
skewers or strong toothpicks; grill
prawns 5 minutes or until changed
in colour.
prep + cook time 30 minutes
makes 16
nutritional count per skewer
1.3g total fat (0.2g saturated fat);
130kJ (31 cal); 0.1g
carbohydrate; 4.7g protein;
0.1g fibre

GREEK EGGPLANT DIP

2 large eggplants (aubergine) (1kg), unpeeled
1 tablespoon coarse cooking salt
¼ cup (60ml) olive oil
½ cup (140g) greek-style yogurt
1 medium white onion (150g), grated coarsely
⅓ cup coarsely chopped fresh flat-leaf parsley
2 tablespoons lemon juice
2 cloves garlic, crushed

1 Cut eggplant into 1cm slices. Place in colander, sprinkle with salt; stand 30 minutes. Rinse eggplant under cold water; drain on absorbent paper.

2 Preheat grill.

3 Brush both sides of eggplant with oil; grill, in batches, until browned both sides and tender. When cool enough to handle remove skin from eggplant.

4 Process eggplant with remaining ingredients until combined. Refrigerate 3 hours or overnight.

prep + cook time 45 minutes (+ standing and refrigeration) **makes** 1½ cups
nutritional count per teaspoon 2.3g total fat (0.6g saturated fat); 125kJ (30 cal); 0.4g carbohydrate; 1.9g protein; 0.1g fibre
Serve dip with fresh crusty bread. Dip can be made three days ahead; store, covered, in the refrigerator.

 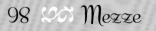

ROSEWATER AND SESAME CHICKEN DRUMETTES

20 chicken drumettes and wings (1.4kg)
2 tablespoons brown sugar
⅓ cup (80ml) rosewater
1 tablespoon olive oil
½ teaspoon ground allspice
2 teaspoons sesame seeds

1 Using small sharp knife pierce chicken all over. Combine chicken, sugar, rosewater, oil and spice in large bowl. Cover; refrigerate 3 hours or overnight.
2 Preheat oven to 220°C/200°C fan-forced.
3 Place chicken on oiled wire rack over large baking dish; pour over any remaining marinade, sprinkle with seeds. Roast chicken, uncovered, basting with pan juices occasionally, 30 minutes or until cooked through.

prep + cook time 35 minutes (+ refrigeration)
makes 20
nutritional count per drumette 5.3g total fat (1.4g saturated fat); 330kJ (79 cal); 1.3g carbohydrate; 6.8g protein; 0g fibre

SPINACH AND FETA TRIANGLES

2 teaspoons olive oil
3 green onions, chopped finely
250g baby spinach leaves
250g feta cheese, crumbled
2 tablespoons finely chopped
   fresh flat-leaf parsley
1 tablespoon finely chopped fresh dill
1 egg
24 sheets filo pastry
150g ghee or butter, melted

1 Heat oil in large frying pan, add onion; cook, stirring, until onion is softened. Add spinach; cook, stirring, until spinach is wilted. Remove from heat. When cool enough to handle, squeeze excess moisture from spinach; chop coarsely.

2 Combine spinach mixture in medium bowl with cheese, herbs and egg.

3 Preheat oven to 200°C/180°C fan-forced. Oil oven trays; line with baking paper.

4 Brush 1 sheet of pastry with ghee; top with a second sheet and brush with ghee. Cut layered sheets into 4 strips lengthways. Place rounded teaspoons of spinach mixture at one end of each strip. Fold one corner of pastry diagonally over filling to form a triangle. Continue folding to end of strip, retaining triangular shape. Brush triangles with a little ghee. Repeat to make a total of 48 triangles.

5 Place triangles on trays. Bake about 15 minutes or until browned lightly.

prep + cook time 1 hour 30 minutes
makes 48
nutritional count per triangle 4.8g total fat (3g saturated fat); 280kJ (67 cal); 3.9g carbohydrate; 1.9g protein; 0.3g fibre
You need to buy a 375g packet of filo pastry. To prevent pastry drying out, cover with plastic wrap or a damp tea towel until ready to use. Uncooked triangles are suitable to freeze. Ghee browns the pastry more evenly than butter.

BEETROOT AND YOGURT DIP

500g beetroot
½ cup (140g) greek-style yogurt
1 clove garlic, crushed
2 tablespoons lemon juice
2 tablespoons coarsely chopped fresh mint

1 Preheat oven to 200°C/180°C fan-forced. Oil oven tray; line with baking paper.
2 Wash beetroot well, cut off leaves. Place unpeeled beetroot on oven tray. Roast about 1 hour or until tender. When beetroot are cool enough to handle, peel and chop coarsely; cool.
3 Process beetroot. Add remaining ingredients; process until smooth. Serve beetroot dip with torn pieces of heated pitta bread.

prep + cook time 1 hour 30 minutes **makes** 1⅓ cups
nutritional count per teaspoon 0.2g total fat (0.1g saturated fat); 25kJ (6 cal); 0.8g carbohydrate; 0.3g protein; 0.2g fibre
Beetroot dip can be made up to two days ahead; store, covered, in the refrigerator.

CHILLI TOMATO

¼ cup coarsely chopped fresh flat-leaf parsley
2 cloves garlic, crushed
½ teaspoon dried chilli flakes
2 tablespoons olive oil
4 large egg tomatoes (360g), sliced thickly

1 Combine parsley, garlic and chilli in small bowl.
2 Heat oil in large frying pan, carefully add tomato in a single layer; cook, over high heat, 2 minutes. Turn tomato, sprinkle with parsley mixture; cook, shaking pan occasionally, about 1 minute or until tomato is caramelised but still holding its shape.
3 Transfer to serving plate; drizzle with pan juices.

prep + cook time 15 minutes **serves** 6
nutritional count per serving 6.2g total fat (0.9g saturated fat); 276kJ (66 cal); 1.5g carbohydrate; 0.7g protein; 1.1g fibre
Take care when adding tomato to pan as it may splatter. Tomato is best cooked just before serving.

GRILLED FETA

200g feta cheese
2 teaspoons olive oil
½ teaspoon sweet paprika
1 loaf ciabatta bread (440g), cut into
   1cm slices
¼ cup (60ml) olive oil, extra
2 teaspoons coarsely chopped fresh
   oregano leaves

1 Preheat grill.
2 Pat cheese dry with absorbent paper. Place cheese on oven tray; brush top and sides with combined oil and paprika. Grill cheese until browned lightly.

3 Lightly brush both sides of bread with extra oil. Toast bread on heated oiled grill plate (or grill or barbecue) until browned both sides.
4 Sprinkle warm cheese with oregano; serve with toasted bread.

prep + cook time 20 minutes **serves** 8
nutritional count per serving 15.2g total fat (5.2g saturated fat); 1150kJ (275 cal); 24.7g carbohydrate; 9.1g protein; 1.6g fibre
Any thick crusty-style bread can be used. Do not line oven tray with baking paper as it may burn during grilling.

LABNE

You need 25cm piece cheesecloth for this recipe; it is available from fabric stores and some kitchenware shops.

2 cups (560g) greek-style yogurt
1½ teaspoons fine table salt
1 tablespoon extra virgin olive oil
½ teaspoon dried chilli flakes
1 tablespoon coarsely chopped fresh
   coriander
1 tablespoon coarsely chopped fresh mint

1 Combine yogurt and salt in medium bowl. Place a 12cm diameter strainer over bowl. Rinse cheesecloth in hot water; wring out then line strainer. Place yogurt into strainer; cover with plastic wrap. Refrigerate at least 24 hours to allow to drain.
2 Turn labne onto serving plate, remove cheesecloth; drizzle labne with oil, sprinkle with chilli, coriander and mint.

prep time 10 minutes (+ refrigeration) **serves** 8
nutritional count per serving 7.2g total fat (3.5g saturated fat); 439kJ (105 cal); 6.3g carbohydrate; 3.9g protein; 0g fibre
Labne can be drained longer than 24 hours, in fact, 48 hours is better; the longer it is drained the firmer it will become.

SARDINES WITH CAPER AND PARSLEY TOPPING

8 sardines (360g), cleaned
⅓ cup (50g) self-raising flour
½ teaspoon sweet paprika
olive oil, for shallow-frying
caper and parsley topping
2 tablespoons rinsed, drained baby capers,
   chopped finely
1 clove garlic, crushed
¼ cup finely chopped fresh flat-leaf parsley
2 teaspoons finely grated lemon rind
2 teaspoons lemon juice

1 Make caper and parsley topping.
2 To butterfly sardines, cut through the underside
of the fish to the tail. Break backbone at tail; peel
away backbone. Trim sardines.
3 Coat fish in combined flour and paprika; shake
away excess. Heat oil in large frying pan; shallow-
fry fish, in batches, until cooked through, drain on
absorbent paper.
4 Sprinkle fish with caper and parsley topping.
Serve with lemon wedges, if you like.
caper and parsley topping Combine
ingredients in small bowl.

prep + cook time 45 minutes **serves** 8
nutritional count per serving 4.6g total fat
(0.9g saturated fat); 376kJ (90 cal); 4.8g
carbohydrate; 7.1g protein; 0.5g fibre
*The caper and parsley topping is best made on the
day of serving; store, covered, in the refrigerator until
ready to use.*

 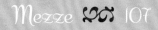

PIDE

basic pide dough Combine 7g yeast, 1 teaspoon sugar, ⅔ cup warm water and 2 tablespoons warm milk in jug. Stand in warm place until frothy. Place ½ cup plain flour in bowl; whisk in yeast mixture. Cover; stand in warm place 1 hour. Stir 1½ cups plain flour and 1 teaspoon salt into yeast mixture with 1 tablespoon olive oil. Knead dough on floured surface until smooth. Place in oiled bowl, cover; stand in warm place 1 hour. Make pide. Or, preheat oven to 240°C/220°C fan-forced. Roll dough into 35cm oval; place dough on baking paper. Make indents with finger and brush over 1 tablespoon olive oil; sprinkle with 2 teaspoons black sesame seeds. Heat oven tray; lift dough onto tray on paper; bake pide about 15 minutes.
prep + cook time 30 minutes (+ standing) **serves** 8
nutritional count per serving 5.6g total fat (0.8g saturated fat); 736kJ (176 cal); 26g carbohydrate; 4.4g protein; 1.6g fibre

egg and cheese pide Preheat oven to 240°C/220°C fan-forced. Divide 1 quantity basic pide dough into three pieces; roll each piece to 12cm x 30cm. Brush edges of dough with water; fold 2cm border around edges of dough, press down firmly. Fold in corners to make oval shape. Heat oven trays in oven for 3 minutes. Quickly place pide on hot trays; bake 5 minutes. Remove from oven; press centre of pide down to flatten. Whisk 3 eggs with 90g coarsely grated haloumi cheese and 1 finely chopped green onion in large jug. Pour into the cavities of the pide. Bake 10 minutes or until set. Cut each pide into eight slices; serve with lemon wedges.
prep + cook time 25 minutes **serves** 8
nutritional count per serving 9.5g total fat (2.7g saturated fat); 970kJ (232 cal); 26.3g carbohydrate; 9.3g protein; 1.6g fibre

lamb and tomato pide Preheat oven to 240°C/220°C fan-forced. Heat 1 tablespoon olive oil in pan; cook 1 chopped brown onion and 1 clove crushed garlic. Add 300g lamb mince, 1 teaspoon each ground cinnamon, cumin and smoked paprika and ½ teaspoon cayenne pepper; cook until lamb is browned. Stir in 1 tablespoon chopped fresh coriander; cool. Divide 1 quantity basic dough into three; roll each piece to 12cm x 30cm. Spread filling across centre of each piece, leaving 2cm border. Brush edges with water; fold and press around dough. Fold corners to make oval shape. Heat oven trays 3 minutes, place pide on trays; bake 10 minutes. Sprinkle with 1 chopped tomato; bake 5 minutes.

prep + cook time 35 minutes
serves 8
nutritional count per serving 10.5g total fat (2.4g saturated fat); 1087kJ (260 cal); 27.5g carbohydrate; 12.6g protein; 2.2g fibre

spinach and feta pide Preheat oven to 240°C/220°C fan-forced. Boil, steam or microwave 300g spinach until wilted. Rinse, drain then squeeze out excess water; shred spinach finely. Combine spinach, 100g crumbled feta cheese and 90g coarsely grated haloumi cheese in medium bowl. Divide 1 quantity basic dough into three; roll each to 12cm x 30cm. Spread filling across centre of each piece, leaving 2cm border. Brush edges with water; fold and press around dough. Fold corners to make oval shape. Heat oven trays 3 minutes, place pide on trays; bake 15 minutes. Cut each pide into eight slices.

prep + cook time 25 minutes
serves 8
nutritional count per serving 10.5g total fat (4g saturated fat); 1028kJ (246 cal); 26.5g carbohydrate; 9.9g protein; 2.6g fibre

pumpkin and feta pide Preheat oven to 240°C/220°C fan-forced. Boil, steam or microwave 200g chopped pumpkin until tender; drain, cool. Combine pumpkin, 100g chopped feta cheese and ½ cup coarsely grated mozzarella cheese in medium bowl. Divide 1 quantity basic dough into three; roll each to 12cm x 30cm. Spread filling across centre of each piece, leaving 2cm border. Brush edges with water; fold and press around dough. Fold corners to make oval shape. Heat oven trays 3 minutes, place pide on trays; bake 15 minutes. Top with 1 tablespoon finely chopped fresh flat-leaf parsley. Cut each pide into eight slices.

prep + cook time 30 minutes
serves 8
nutritional count per serving 10.2g total fat (3.9g saturated fat); 1020kJ (244 cal); 26.7g carbohydrate; 9.1g protein; 1.9g fibre

ZUCCHINI FRITTERS WITH SKORDALIA

4 medium zucchini (courgettes) (480g)
2 teaspoons coarse cooking salt
peanut oil, for deep-frying
skordalia
4 slices stale white sandwich bread (180g), crusts removed
4 cloves garlic, crushed
½ cup (125ml) olive oil
1 tablespoon lemon juice
1 tablespoon water, approximately
batter
1 cup (150g) self-raising flour
¾ cup (180ml) warm water
1 tablespoon olive oil
1 egg yolk

1 Make skordalia.
2 Cut zucchini into 1cm diagonal slices. Place zucchini in colander, sprinkle with salt; stand 30 minutes. Rinse zucchini under cold water; drain on absorbent paper.
3 Make batter.
4 Heat oil in large saucepan. Dip zucchini into batter, carefully lower into hot oil; cook zucchini until browned and crisp; drain on absorbent paper.
5 Serve zucchini fritters with skordalia.
skordalia Briefly dip bread into a bowl of cold water, then gently squeeze out the water. Blend or process bread and garlic until combined. With motor operating, gradually add oil, juice and enough of the water, in a thin steady stream, until mixture is smooth wand thick. Transfer to serving bowl.
batter Sift flour into medium bowl; whisk in combined remaining ingredients until smooth. Stand batter 10 minutes. If batter thickens too much, whisk in a little extra water to give it a coating consistency.

prep + cook time 1 hour (+ standing)
serves 6
nutritional count per serving 28g total fat (4.2g saturated fat); 1601kJ (383 cal); 26.5g carbohydrate; 5.4g protein; 3g fibre
Zucchini fritters are best made just before serving. Skordalia is best made on the day of serving; keep, covered, in the refrigerator.

mini baked herb ricotta

mini chicken souvlakia

MINI BAKED HERB RICOTTA

250g ricotta cheese
1 egg
1 tablespoon finely chopped fresh flat-leaf
    parsley
1 teaspoon finely chopped fresh thyme
1 clove garlic, crushed

1 Preheat oven to 180°C/160°C fan-forced.
Oil 18 holes of two 12-hole
(1½-tablespoons/20ml) mini muffin pans.
2 Blend or process ingredients until smooth.
Divide mixture into pan holes. Bake about 20
minutes or until browned lightly.

prep + cook time 30 minutes **makes** 18
nutritional count per ricotta 1.9g total fat (1.1g
saturated fat); 105kJ (25 cal); 0.2g carbohydrate;
1.8g protein; 0g fibre
*Serve mini baked ricottas warm or cold. Recipe
can be made a day ahead; store, covered, in the
refrigerator.*

MINI CHICKEN SOUVLAKIA

1kg chicken thigh fillets
2 tablespoons olive oil
2 tablespoons lemon juice
⅓ cup finely chopped fresh mint
2 cloves garlic, crushed
1½ teaspoons smoked paprika

1 Trim any fat from chicken; cut chicken into 2cm
thick strips. Combine chicken in medium bowl with
remaining ingredients. Thread chicken onto 20
bamboo skewers; cover, refrigerate 3 hours or
overnight.
2 Cook skewers on heated oiled grill plate (or grill
or barbecue) until browned and cooked through.
Serve with lemon wedges, if you like.

prep + cook time 35 minutes (+ refrigeration)
makes 20
nutritional count per skewer 5.4g total fat
(1.4g saturated fat); 364kJ (87 cal); 0.1g
carbohydrate; 9.4g protein; 0.1g fibre
*Soak the skewers in cold water for at least an
hour before using to prevent them from scorching
during cooking. For optimum flavour, marinate the
chicken overnight.*

TURKISH LAMB FILO CIGARS

2 tablespoons olive oil
1 medium brown onion (150g), chopped
 finely
2 cloves garlic, crushed
2 teaspoons ground allspice
2 teaspoons ground coriander
1½ teaspoons ground cinnamon
1 teaspoon ground cumin
300g lean lamb mince
1 tablespoon lemon juice
6 sheets filo pastry
100g butter, melted
mint yogurt
½ cup (140g) greek-style yogurt
1 tablespoon finely chopped fresh mint

1 Heat oil in medium frying pan, add onion
and garlic; cook, stirring, until onion softens.
Add spices; cook, stirring, until fragrant. Add
mince; cook, stirring until mince is cooked
through. Stir in juice; cool.
2 Preheat oven to 220°C/200°C fan-forced.
Oil oven tray; line with baking paper.
3 Brush 1 sheet of pastry with butter; top with
two more sheets, brushing each with butter.
Cut layered sheets into 8 rectangles. Press
1 tablespoon of lamb mixture into a log shape
along one long end of each rectangle. Roll
pastry over filling; fold in sides then
roll up to form a cigar shape. Repeat to make
a total of 16 cigar shapes.
4 Place cigars, about 2cm apart, on oven tray,
brush with remaining butter. Bake about 15
minutes or until browned lightly.
5 Meanwhile, make mint yogurt.
6 Serve warm cigars with mint yogurt.
mint yogurt Combine ingredients in
small bowl.

prep + cook time 1 hour 30 minutes
makes 16
nutritional count per piece 9.4g total fat
(4.7g saturated fat); 510kJ (122 cal); 4.3g
carbohydrate; 5g protein; 0.3g fibre
*To prevent pastry from drying out, cover with
plastic wrap then top with a damp tea-towel
until ready to use. Uncooked filo cigars are
suitable to freeze.*

BROAD BEAN DIP

500g frozen broad beans
1 clove garlic, crushed
1 teaspoon ground cumin
½ teaspoon smoked paprika
2 tablespoons olive oil
1 tablespoon lemon juice
1 tablespoon finely chopped fresh mint
1 tablespoon olive oil, extra
¼ teaspoon smoked paprika, extra

1 Cook beans in medium saucepan of boiling water until tender; drain, reserving some of the cooking liquid. When cool enough to handle, peel away grey-coloured outer shells from beans.
2 Blend or process beans with garlic, spices, oil, juice, mint and enough of the reserved cooking liquid until mixture is smooth.
3 Serve dip drizzled with extra oil and sprinkled with extra paprika.

prep + cook time 20 minutes **makes** 1¾ cups
nutritional count per teaspoon 0.7g total fat (0.1g saturated fat); 29kJ (7 cal); 0.1g carbohydrate; 0.2g protein; 0.2g fibre
Dip can be made a day ahead; store, covered, in the refrigerator.

CHAR-GRILLED BANANA CHILLIES

4 red banana chillies (500g)
1 tablespoon white wine vinegar
1 tablespoon olive oil
2 teaspoons finely chopped fresh flat-leaf
  parsley

1 Preheat grill.
2 Cook whole chillies under hot grill until blistered and blackened. Cover chillies with plastic or paper for 5 minutes; peel away skin.
3 Arrange whole chillies on serving plate; drizzle with combined vinegar, oil and parsley.

prep + cook time 30 minutes **serves** 4
nutritional count per serving 4.8g total fat (0.6g saturated fat); 238kJ (57 cal); 2.1g carbohydrate; 0.8g protein; 1.4g fibre
Recipe can be made a day ahead; store, covered, in the refrigerator.

DOLMADES

2 tablespoons olive oil
2 medium brown onions (300g), chopped
   finely
150g lean lamb mince
¾ cup (150g) white long-grain rice
2 tablespoons pine nuts
½ cup finely chopped fresh flat-leaf parsley
2 tablespoons finely chopped fresh dill
2 tablespoons finely chopped fresh mint
2 tablespoons lemon juice
1 cup (250ml) water
500g preserved vine leaves
1 cup (250ml) water, extra
1 tablespoon lemon juice, extra
¾ cup (200g) yogurt

1 Heat oil in large saucepan, add onion; cook, stirring, until softened. Add mince; cook, stirring, until mince is browned. Stir in rice and pine nuts. Add herbs, juice and the water. Bring to the boil; reduce heat, simmer, covered, about 10 minutes or until water is absorbed and rice is partially cooked. Cool.
2 Rinse vine leaves in cold water. Drop leaves into a large saucepan of boiling water, in batches, for a few seconds, transfer to colander; rinse under cold water, drain well.

3 Place a vine leaf, smooth side down on bench, trim large stem. Place a heaped teaspoon of rice mixture in centre. Fold stem end and sides over filling; roll up firmly. Line medium heavy-based saucepan with a few vine leaves, place rolls, close together, seam side down on leaves.
4 Pour the extra water over top of rolls; cover rolls with any remaining vine leaves. Place a plate on top of the leaves to keep rolls under the water during cooking. Cover pan tightly, bring to the boil; reduce heat, simmer, over very low heat, 1½ hours. Remove from heat; stand, covered about 2 hours or until all the liquid has been absorbed.
5 Serve with combined extra juice and yogurt.

prep + cook time 3 hours (+ standing)
serves 10
nutritional count per serving 7.6g total fat (1.6g saturated fat); 690kJ (165 cal); 14.9g carbohydrate; 7.7g protein; 3.2g fibre
Use any torn or damaged leaves to line the base of the pan and to cover the rolls. If you don't have enough vine leaves to cover the rolls in the pan, use a circle of baking paper, then top with the plate. Dolmades are best made a day ahead; store, covered, in the refrigerator.

MINI FALAFEL WITH TOMATO SALSA

400g can chickpeas, rinsed, drained
1 small white onion (80g), chopped finely
½ cup finely chopped fresh flat-leaf parsley
2 tablespoons finely chopped fresh
    coriander
2 teaspoons ground cumin
2 teaspoons ground coriander
1 tablespoon finely grated lemon rind
1 teaspoon salt
¼ cup (35g) plain flour
peanut oil, for deep-frying
tomato salsa
1 medium egg tomato (75g), chopped finely
1 tablespoon coarsely chopped fresh
    coriander
1 tablespoon olive oil

1 To make falafel, blend or process chickpeas, onion, herbs, spices, rind and salt until coarsely chopped. Add flour; process until mixture forms a paste. Transfer mixture to medium bowl; cover, refrigerate 1 hour.
2 Make tomato salsa.
3 Shape falafel mixture between two teaspoons into oval shapes. Heat oil in medium deep frying pan; cook falafel, in batches, until browned. Drain on absorbent paper.
4 Serve falafel with tomato salsa.
tomato salsa Combine ingredients in small bowl.

prep + cook time 1 hour 30 minutes
(+ refrigeration) **makes** 32
nutritional count per serving 1.4g total fat
(0.2g saturated fat); 105kJ (25 cal); 2.1g
carbohydrate; 0.7g protein; 0.6g fibre
*Falafel can be made a day ahead; store, covered,
in the refrigerator.*

GREEK MEATBALLS

1 tablespoon olive oil
1 medium brown onion (150g),
  chopped finely
2 cloves garlic, crushed
1kg lean lamb mince
1 egg
1½ cups (100g) stale breadcrumbs
2 tablespoons lemon juice
¼ cup finely chopped fresh flat-leaf parsley
¼ cup finely chopped fresh mint
⅓ cup (50g) plain flour
olive oil, extra, for shallow-frying

1 Heat oil in medium frying pan, add onion
and garlic; cook, stirring, until onion is softened. Cool.
2 Combine onion mixture with mince, egg,
breadcrumbs, juice, parsley and mint in large bowl.
Cover, refrigerate 1 hour.
3 Roll level tablespoons of mixture into balls;
toss balls in flour, shake away excess. Heat extra
oil in same cleaned pan; shallow-fry meatballs,
in batches, until cooked through. Drain on
absorbent paper.
4 Serve meatballs with yogurt, if you like.

prep + cook time 1 hour (+ refrigeration)
makes 50
nutritional count per meatball 4.7g total fat
(1.1g saturated fat); 297kJ (71 cal); 2.3g
carbohydrate; 4.7g protein; 0.2g fibre
*The oil should be very hot before cooking the
meatballs. Beef or veal mince can also be used
in this recipe.*

GLOSSARY

allspice also called pimento or jamaican pepper. Available whole or ground.

almonds

flaked paper-thin slices.

slivered thin lengthways-cut pieces.

artichoke, globe the bud of a large plant from the thistle family; has tough, petal-shaped leaves and an inedible prickly choke that should be discarded leaving the tender artichoke heart. Artichoke hearts are also available in brine in cans or in glass jars.

beans

broad also called fava, windsor and horse beans. Fresh and frozen forms should be peeled twice, discarding the outer long green pod and the tough beige-green inner shell.

white in this book, some recipes may simply call for 'white beans', a generic term we use for cannellini, haricot, navy or great northern beans – all of which can be substituted for each other.

beetroot also known as red beets or beets; a firm, round root vegetable.

bread

brioche can be made in the shape of a loaf or roll. A rich, French yeast bread with a dark, golden, flaky crust; typically baked in a fluted pan.

ciabatta in italian, the word means 'slipper', which is the traditional shape of this white bread with a crisp crust.

pitta also known as lebanese bread; a pocket bread sold in large, flat pieces that separate into two thin rounds. Also available in small thick pieces called pocket pitta.

sourdough made by using a small amount of 'starter dough' (dough from a previous batch, containing a yeast culture). Part of the resulting dough is then saved to use as the starter dough next time.

turkish also known as pide; comes in long (about 45cm) flat loaves as well as individual rounds. Made from wheat flour and sprinkled with sesame seeds or kalonji.

breadcrumbs

packaged fine-textured, crunchy, purchased white breadcrumbs.

stale one- or two-day-old bread made into crumbs by blending or processing.

butter use salted or unsalted (sweet) butter; 125g is equal to one stick (4oz).

caperberries fruit formed after the caper buds have flowered; caperberries are pickled, usually with stalks intact.

capers the grey-green buds of a warm climate (usually Mediterranean) shrub; sold dried and salted or pickled in a vinegar brine. Capers should be rinsed well before using.

capsicum also called bell pepper or pepper. Discard seeds and membranes before use.

cayenne pepper a long, thin-fleshed, very hot red chilli usually sold dried and ground.

cheese

blue mould-treated cheeses mottled with blue veining. Varieties include firm and crumbly stilton types to mild, creamy brie-like cheeses.

bocconcini baby mozzarella; walnut-sized, delicate, semi-soft, white cheese. Spoils rapidly so must be kept under refrigeration, in brine, for 2 days at most.

cream cheese also known as Philly or Philadelphia, a soft, cows-milk cheese.

feta a crumbly textured goat or sheep milk cheese with a sharp, salty taste.

goats made from goat milk; has an earthy, strong taste. Available as soft and firm, and in various shapes and sizes, sometimes rolled in ash or herbs.

haloumi a firm, cream-coloured sheep-milk cheese matured in brine; can be grilled or fried, briefly, without breaking down. Should be eaten while still warm as it becomes tough and rubbery on cooling.

mascarpone a cultured cream product made similarly to yogurt. It's a buttery-rich, cream-like cheese made from cows milk. Ivory-coloured, soft and delicate, with the texture of softened butter.

mozzarella a soft, spun-curd cheese. It has a low melting point and elastic texture when heated; adds texture rather than flavour.

ricotta the name for this soft, white, cows-milk cheese roughly translates as 'cooked again'. It's made from whey, a by-product of other cheese-making, to which fresh milk and acid are added. Ricotta is a sweet, moist cheese with a slightly grainy texture.

romano a hard cheese with excellent keeping qualities. Made from sheep milk, this straw-coloured cheese has a grainy texture and is mainly used for grating. Substitute with parmesan.

parmesan also known as parmigiano; a hard, grainy, cows-milk cheese. The curd is salted in brine for a month before being aged for up to two years in humid conditions.

chervil also known as cicily; a herb with a mild fennel flavour.

chickpeas also called garbanzos, hummus or channa; an irregularly round, sandy-coloured legume.

chilli

banana also known as wax chillies or hungarian peppers; are almost as mild as capsicum but have a distinctively sweet sharpness to their taste. Sold in varying degrees of ripeness, they can be found in pale olive green, yellow and red varieties at greengrocers and most supermarkets.

flakes dried, deep-red, dehydrated chilli slices and whole seeds.

long red available both fresh and dried; a generic term used for any moderately hot, long (6cm to 8cm), thin chilli.

thai red also known as 'scuds'; small, very hot and bright red in colour.

chorizo a sausage of Spanish origin, made of coarsely ground pork and highly seasoned with garlic and chillies.

coppa a salted dried sausage made from the neck or shoulder of pork. Is deep red in colour and is available both mild and spicy.

coriander also known as pak chee, cilantro or chinese parsley; a bright-green leafy herb with a pungent flavour. Stems and roots of coriander may also be used; wash well before chopping. Coriander is also available ground or as seeds, but these are no substitute for fresh coriander as the tastes are very different.

cream we used fresh cream, also known as pure cream and pouring cream, unless otherwise stated. Minimum fat content 35%.

crème fraîche mature fermented cream having a slightly tangy, nutty flavour and velvety texture. Minimum fat content 35%.

cumin also known as zeera or comino.

eggplant purple-skinned vegetable also known as aubergine. Can also be purchased char-grilled, packed in oil, in jars.

fennel also known as finocchio or anise; a white to very pale green-white, firm, crisp, roundish vegetable about 8-12cm in diameter. The bulb has a slightly sweet, anise flavour but the leaves (fronds) have a much stronger taste. Also the name given to dried seeds having a licorice flavour.

fish fillets, firm white any firm white boneless fish fillet – blue eye, bream, ling, swordfish, whiting or sea perch are all good choices. Check for any small pieces of bone in fillets and use tweezers to remove them.

flour

plain an all-purpose flour made from wheat.

rice a fine flour made from ground white rice.

self-raising plain flour sifted with baking powder in the proportion of 1 cup flour to
2 teaspoons baking powder.

ghee also known as clarified butter; butter that has had its milk solids removed, so it can be heated to a high temperature without burning.

harissa a moroccan sauce or paste made from dried chillies, cumin, garlic, oil and caraway seeds. Is available from major supermarkets and Middle-Eastern food stores.

lebanese cucumber short, slender and thin-skinned. Probably the most popular variety because of its tender, edible skin, tiny, yielding

seeds and sweet, fresh taste.

lettuce, baby cos also known as romaine lettuce; the traditional caesar salad lettuce. Long, with leaves ranging from dark green on the outside to almost white near the core; the leaves have a stiff centre rib that gives a slight cupping effect to the leaf.

mussels buy from a fish market where there is reliably fresh fish; must be tightly closed when bought, indicating they are alive. Before cooking, scrub the shells with a strong brush and remove the beards; discard any shells that do not open after cooking. Varieties include black and green-lip.

mustard, wholegrain also called seeded. A french-style coarse-grain mustard made from crushed mustard seeds and dijon-style french mustard.

oil

cooking spray we use a cholesterol-free cooking spray made from canola oil.

olive made from ripened olives. Extra virgin and virgin are the best, while extra light or light refers to taste not fat levels.

vegetable from plants rather than animal fats.

olives

anchovy-stuffed green manzanilla medium-sized green or black pickled olives; found at specialty food stores.

feta-stuffed green green olives stuffed with feta cheese.

green those harvested before fully ripened and are, as a rule, denser and more bitter than their black relatives.

kalamata small, sharp-tasting, brine-cured black olives.

ligurian very small black olives with a nutty flavour.

niçoise small black olives.

pimiento-stuffed green a green olive with a lively, briny bitterness and stuffed with a morsel of capsicum, which adds colour.

sicilian dark olive green in colour; can be found almost everywhere olives are sold. Crack but do not seed them, and ensure you to alert your guests to the seeds. Brine-cured sicilian olives

are smooth and fine-skinned, crisp and crunchy to the bite – they have a refreshingly piquant, buttery flavour.

wild available from select delicatessens. Substitute with small ligurian olives if you can't find them.

onion

green also scallion or, incorrectly, shallot; an immature onion picked before the bulb has formed, having a long, green edible stalk.

red also known as spanish, red spanish or bermuda onion; a sweet-flavoured, large, purple-red onion.

shallots also called french shallots, golden shallots or eschalots; small, brown-skinned, elongated members of the onion family. Grows in tight clusters similar to garlic.

spring onions with small white bulbs and long narrow, green leafy tops.

pancetta pork belly that is cured but not smoked; bacon can be substituted.

paprika ground dried sweet red capsicum (bell pepper); there are many types available, including sweet, hot, mild and smoked.

peppercorns, black picked when the berry is not quite ripe, then dried until it shrivels and the skin turns dark brown to black. Strongly flavoured.

pine nuts also known as pignoli; not, in fact, a nut but a small, cream-coloured kernel from pine cones.

pistachio pale green, delicately flavoured nut inside hard off-white shells. To peel, soak shelled nuts in boiling water for about
5 minutes; drain, pat dry with absorbent paper. Rub skins with a cloth to peel.

polenta also known as cornmeal; a flour-like cereal made of dried corn (maize). Also the name of the dish made from it.

pomegranate molasses is thicker, browner and more concentrated than grenadine, the sweet, red pomegranate syrup used in cocktails. Has a tart, fruity quality similar to balsamic vinegar. It is available from Middle-Eastern food stores, specialty food shops and better delicatessens.

prawns also known as shrimp.

prosciutto cured, air-dried, pressed ham. Usually sold thinly sliced.

quail small, delicately flavoured, domestically grown game birds ranging in weight from 250g to 300g; also known as partridge.

quince yellow-skinned fruit with a hard texture and an astringent, tart taste; eaten cooked or as a preserve.

radish a peppery root vegetable related to the mustard plant. The small round red variety is the mildest.

rice

arborio small, round-grain rice, well-suited to absorb a large amount of liquid; especially suitable for risottos.

long-grain elongated grain, remains separate when cooked; most popular steaming rice in South-East Asia.

medium-grain previously sold as Calrose rice; versatile rice that can be substituted for short- or long-grain rice if necessary.

short-grain a fat, almost round-grain rice with a high starch content; tends to clump together when cooked.

roasting nuts put shelled nuts in a baking pan and bake in a hot oven, stirring occasionally, until slightly golden in colour, about 10 minutes.

rocket also known as arugula, rugula and rucola; a peppery-tasting green leaf. Baby rocket leaves, also known as wild rocket, are both smaller and less peppery.

rosewater called gulab in India. An extract made from crushed rose petals; used for its aromatic quality. Available from Middle-Eastern food stores and some delicatessens.

saffron available in strands or ground form; imparts a yellow-orange colour to food once infused. Quality varies greatly; the best is the most expensive spice in the world. Should be stored in the freezer.

sashimi skinless, boneless raw fish pieces certified as safe to eat. Use the freshest, sashimi-quality fish you can find. Raw fish sold as sashimi has to meet stringent guidelines regarding its handling and treatment after leaving the water. We suggest you seek local advice from authorities before eating any raw seafood.

scallops a bivalve mollusc with a fluted shell valve.

sesame seeds black and white are the most common of this small oval seed, but there are red and brown varieties also.

sopressa a semi-hard pork salami typically flavoured with pepper, cloves, cinnamon, nutmeg, rosemary and garlic; hot or mild.

speck also known as cured pork.

spinach also known as english spinach and, incorrectly, silver beet.

squid a type of mollusc; also called calamari. Buy squid hoods to make preparation easier.

sterilising jars place cleaned glass jars on their sides in a large saucepan; cover with cold water. Cover pan, bring to the boil, and boil for 20 minutes. Carefully remove jars from water; drain. Stand jars, top-side up, on a wooden board. The heat from the jars will cause any remaining water to evaporate quickly. Place jars, on wooden board, in a cold oven (do not allow the jars to touch); heat oven temperature to 120°C/100°C fan-forced, then leave jars in oven 30 minutes. Plastic screw-top lids give a good seal (plastic snap-on lids are not airtight enough). Plastic lids must be well washed, rinsed and dried, or put through the dishwasher.

sugar

brown an extremely soft, finely granulated sugar retaining molasses for its characteristic colour and flavour.

caster also known as superfine or finely granulated table sugar.

veal schnitzels a thinly sliced steak available crumbed or plain (uncrumbed); we use plain schnitzel, sometimes called escalopes

unless indicated otherwise.

vine leaves from early spring, fresh grapevine leaves can be found in most specialist greengrocers. Alternatively, cryovac-packed leaves in brine can be found in Middle-Eastern food shops and some delicatessens; these must be rinsed well and dried before using. We used vine leaves in brine; available in jars and packets from supermarkets.

vinegar

balsamic made from trebbiano grapes; it is a deep rich brown colour with a sweet and sour flavour.

cider (apple cider) made from crushed fermented apples.

red wine based on fermented red wine.

sherry made from a blend of wines and left in wood vats to mature, where they develop a rich mellow flavour.

white made from cane sugar.

white wine made from white wine.

watercress also known as winter rocket; one of the cress family, a large group of peppery greens. Highly perishable, so must be used as soon as possible after purchase.

witlof also known as chicory or belgian endive; its cigar-shaped, tightly packed heads have pale, yellow-green tips, and a delicately bitter flavour. Eaten cooked or raw.

yeast a 7g (¼oz) sachet of dried yeast (2 teaspoons) is equal to 15g (½oz) compressed yeast; they can be substituted for each other.

yogurt we used plain, unflavoured yogurt, unless otherwise specified.

zucchini also called courgette; harvested when young, its edible flowers can be stuffed then deep-fried or oven-baked.

CONVERSION CHART

measures

One Australian metric measuring cup holds approximately 250ml; one Australian metric tablespoon holds 20ml; one Australian metric teaspoon holds 5ml.

The difference between one country's measuring cups and another's is within a two- or three-teaspoon variance, and will not affect your cooking results. North America, New Zealand and the United Kingdom use a 15ml tablespoon.

All cup and spoon measurements are level. The most accurate way of measuring dry ingredients is to weigh them. When measuring liquids, use a clear glass or plastic jug with the metric markings.

We use large eggs with an average weight of 60g.

dry measures

METRIC	IMPERIAL
15g	½oz
30g	1oz
60g	2oz
90g	3oz
125g	4oz (¼lb)
155g	5oz
185g	6oz
220g	7oz
250g	8oz (½lb)
280g	9oz
315g	10oz
345g	11oz
375g	12oz (¾lb)
410g	13oz
440g	14oz
470g	15oz
500g	16oz (1lb)
750g	24oz (1½lb)
1kg	32oz (2lb)

liquid measures

METRIC	IMPERIAL
30ml	1 fluid oz
60ml	2 fluid oz
100ml	3 fluid oz
125ml	4 fluid oz
150ml	5 fluid oz (¼ pint/1 gill)
190ml	6 fluid oz
250ml	8 fluid oz
300ml	10 fluid oz (½ pint)
500ml	16 fluid oz
600ml	20 fluid oz (1 pint)
1000ml (1 litre)	1¾ pints

length measures

3mm	⅛in
6mm	¼in
1cm	½in
2cm	¾in
2.5cm	1in
5cm	2in
6cm	2½in
8cm	3in
10cm	4in
13cm	5in
15cm	6in
18cm	7in
20cm	8in
23cm	9in
25cm	10in
28cm	11in
30cm	12in (1ft)

oven temperatures

These oven temperatures are only a guide for conventional ovens. For fan-forced ovens, check the manufacturer's manual.

	°C (CELSIUS)	°F (FAHRENHEIT)	GAS MARK
Very slow	120	250	½
Slow	150	275-300	1-2
Moderately slow	160	325	3
Moderate	180	350-375	4-5
Moderately hot	200	400	6
Hot	220	425-450	7-8
Very hot	240	475	9

INDEX

This book is published in 2015 by Bounty Books, based on materials licensed to it by Bauer Media Books, Australia First published in 2009 by Bauer Media Books.

Bauer Media Books is a division of Bauer Media Pty Limited. 54 Park St, Sydney; GPO Box 4088, Sydney, NSW 2001, Australia

phone (+61) 2 9282 8618; fax (+61) 2 9126 3702 www.awwcookbooks.com.au

BAUER MEDIA BOOKS

General manager Christine Whiston
Editor-in-chief Susan Tomnay
Creative director Hieu Chi Nguyen
Art director & designer Hannah Blackmore
Senior editor Stephanie Kistner
Food director Pamela Clark
Recipe development Clara Laboff, Rebecca Squadrito, Louise Patniotis
Sales & rights director Brian Cearnes
Marketing manager Bridget Cody
Senior business analyst Rebecca Varela
Circulation manager Jarna Mclean
Operations manager David Scotto
Production manager Victoria Jefferys

Photographer Ian Wallace
Stylist Louise Pickford
Food preparation Amal Webster

The publishers would like to thank the following for props used in photography:
Alfresco Emporium; Chee Soon & Fitzgerald; Hub Furniture; Mud Australia; Papaya; Teranova Tile Boutique; Thonet Australia; Village Living Pty Ltd.

Published and distributed in the United Kingdom by Bounty Books, a division of Octopus Publishing Group Ltd An Hachette UK Company www.hachette.co.uk

Carmelite House, 50 Victoria Embankment, London, EC4Y 0DZ www.octopusbooks.co.uk

International foreign language rights, Brian Cearnes, Bauer Media Books bcearnes@bauer-media.com.au

A CIP catalogue record for this book is available from the British Library

ISBN: 978-0-7537-2987-8

© Bauer Media Pty Ltd 2009
ABN 18 053 273 546

Printed and bound in China

10 9 8 7 6 5 4 3 2 1